From one pageant winner to another, Christina Meredith's life experience and real-life Cinderella story are beyond inspirational to me, and I'm so proud of her. She is an overcomer like few I've ever read about. But what impresses me the most is her desire to transform the foster care system and use her challenges to better the next generation.

Kristen Dalton-Wolfe, bestselling author and former Miss USA

Christina Meredith's story, which she tells with unique courage, follows a young woman's rise out of vulnerability, homelessness, and abuse to become a soldier, leader, and pillar in her community. Christina's spirited and empathetic soul shines through every page. She will leave a big and beautiful mark on this broken world.

Jason Jones, author, activist, film producer

It's been said that "God can't use someone greatly until they've hurt deeply." Because of this principle, Christina Meredith is destined to make the world a better place. In circumstances that would have turned others toward bitterness and despair, Christina has managed to turn the unspeakable heartache of a horrible childhood into hope and a blessing—not only for other victims of abuse but for anyone who reads her book. Passionately told, her compelling life story is one of triumph over pain while clinging to the perfect love of her heavenly Father. She's a true inspiration!

David McQuade, founder of Z Music Television and former president of Gener8Xion Entertainment

Christina Meredith has written a memoir that is one-of-a-kind in that it is not just the end result of a soul-crushing childhood; it is the beginning of Christina's unstoppable mission to inspire and encourage the up-and-coming generation. In spirit, mind, and heart, Christina is capable of positively impacting humanity—and just watch: she will.

Elizabeth Kennedy Ryzewicz, media producer

Christina Meredith is a remarkable woman, and *CinderGirl* is an inspirational book. Christina is not a victim of her circumstances—the awfulness of abuse, neglect, and foster care—she is a survivor, a heroine in the story of her own life. Reading this beautifully written and impassioned book will lift up many people and turn them to the light of their own potential, to understand that their past does not determine their future; their present is where they chart their course. I tip my hat to a high achiever against great odds!

Peter Samuelson, president, www.firststar.org

Christina Meredith has the one-of-a-kind courage and strength that I rarely see in up-and-coming leaders. All that Ms. Meredith has overcome, as she has masterfully written in her heartbreaking memoir, is matched only by her unwavering commitment, and ability, to dramatically impact our world for the better.

Brad Freeman, founding partner, Freeman Spogli & Co.

Christina Meredith's story of her upbringing and rise to where she is now is absolutely amazing. The amount of courage possessed in her soul, body, and mind to write a memoir with such passion is truly remarkable. Reading her book without a flood of emotions is impossible for anyone with any compassion. I've known Christina for a number of years. From the first time I met her, I've seen that she is full of humility and compassion toward others. This book is a small stepping-stone to and a glimpse at where she will go in the future.

Tim Ockler, educator

Cinder Girl

Cinder Girl

MY JOURNEY OUT OF THE ASHES TO A LIFE OF HOPE

A MEMOIR

CHRISTINA MEREDITH

ZONDERVAN

CinderGirl
Copyright © 2019 by Christina Meredith

Requests for information should be addressed to:
Zondervan, *3900 Sparks Dr. SE, Grand Rapids, Michigan 49546*

ISBN 978-0-310-34893-1 (softcover)

ISBN 978-0-310-35543-4 (audio)

ISBN 978-0-310-34895-5 (ebook)

Published in association with Dupree Miller & Associates, 4311 Oak Lawn Avenue, #650, Dallas, TX 75219.

Cover design: James W. Hall IV
Cover photography: Amber Nicole Portrait
Interior design: Kait Lamphere

Printed in the United States of America

19 20 21 22 23 24 25 /LSC/ 15 14 13 12 11 10 9 8 7 6 5 4 3 2 1

To my beloved brother in Christ, Jay—
my biggest fan.
Without you,
I never would have made anything of myself.
I'd give anything for you to be here.
I love you, and I miss you.

Contents

Author's Note

This is a work of nonfiction. The events and experiences detailed herein are all true and have been faithfully rendered as I have remembered them, to the best of my ability. Some names, identities, and circumstances have been changed in order to protect the anonymity of the individuals involved. Though conversations come from my keen recollection of them, they are not written to represent word-for-word documentation; rather, I have retold them in a way that evokes the real feeling and meaning of what was said, in keeping with the true essence of the mood and spirit of the event.

Foreword

At one point, Christina Meredith screamed questions many of us have asked: "How could my Father in heaven allow me to suffer this way? God, are you there?"

I remember the email. It was from a friend I hadn't seen for some time. He told me about a young woman who had aged out of the foster care system and who had won Ms. California. But she was homeless in LA and needed a place to stay until she got on her feet. "Do you know anyone who can help her?" he asked.

It hit me in a way I've learned to listen to, as though God might be speaking to me. For more than a year, my wife, Tori, had been telling me she was feeling more and more of a burden for kids who age out of foster care and who have nowhere to go. Many end up in prostitution, sex slavery, or other horrible situations, as they're too old for the system to help them but not really strong enough to be adults and make their own way. We had made some inroads into that world, and Tori had begun working with some organizations.

We had been asking God to open up opportunities for us to help more foster kids.

I felt this might be the next step. Here was one of those young people Tori was wanting to help. I called my friend and asked if I could speak to the woman who had reached out to him and who would serve as a reference for the young woman who needed help. He put me in touch with Betsy, and we had a long conversation about Christina. She told me her story, and I was moved. I asked her about Christina's trustworthiness and character. Tori and I were considering opening our home to Christina, and since she would be coming into our home with our young daughters, I wanted to make sure all would be okay. She assured me it would. The next step was to interview Christina. After that, it became clear to me that God was leading us to invite Christina to live with us for a while.

What I didn't know was what the next step of her path might be, or how I might be able to help. I felt like there wasn't much I would be able to do for her other than to offer her a place to live while she got on her feet. But at least we could do that much. I had a strange feeling I was supposed to do something more; I just had no idea what that was.

It wasn't long before I found out.

First, Christina's life story is incredible. She endured abuse at the hands of her mother, having been singled out as the "bad sibling" and essentially forced to wait on her family as a domestic servant. She was sexually abused for years by a family member and not given justice by a legal system.

Second, as terrible as this was, God intervened. He had

shown himself to be real, to move on her behalf, to supernaturally speak to a homeless teen living on the street and tell her that one day she would be a leader to other abused homeless children, write a book, and speak to thousands. This inspired me. It reminded me again of what I've seen God do over and over again in what feels like the worst of situations: show himself to be real and come to the aid of the suffering and oppressed.

Third, I quickly learned that Christina was certain that God had spoken to her, that one day she would write a book and use that platform to help foster kids. But she had hit a wall. She had tried to pursue her dream, but time after time an agent and publisher had rejected her. She was at a dead end. She had nowhere to turn and no clue how to get a book published, but she was certain that God would open a door. At that moment, it all made sense to me.

Though I had felt there was nothing I could do for her, it became clear as day. I just wanted to laugh. What a God we have! Here was a young woman who had hit a door slammed shut on her dream of getting a book published, but she hadn't given up on God. She just kept praying. And he just so happens to drop her into the home of someone who knows a little bit about getting a book published and who knows some people who could quickly make this happen.

I just smiled. I remember saying, "This is funny. I had no idea how I might help you, but I can at least do this much. I will connect you with my agent. She'll love your story, and you'll be off and running." I had no doubt.

So here we are, book in hand. It all came true. It has been exciting to watch God fulfill the dream he gave her when she was on the streets—abused, homeless, and helpless. It has been inspiring to see her faith lived out through a difficult journey of trauma healing, closed doors, poverty, success, and multiple restarts with an unwavering commitment to helping those who have suffered as she did. To me, this book and her story reveal the truth of how she is a living example of Paul's description of what God can do with the pain in our life:

> Praise be to the God and Father of our Lord Jesus Christ, the Father of compassion and the God of all comfort, who comforts us in all our troubles, so that we can comfort those in any trouble with the comfort we ourselves receive from God.
>
> *2 Corinthians 1:3–4*

Truly God has done this in Christina's life, and Christina is doing that now. God rescued her from horrible pain and abuse, and God comforted her. And now she is doing the same, comforting others with her story of hope and victory. Her wish for this book—and mine as well—is that it will move you to be part of the same story God is writing for you, no matter which part you find yourself in now. If you are hurting and hopeless, let her story lead you to the God who promises to bring you to a better place and who will do for you what he has done for Christina. Use your experience of suffering to help others who are hurting. There is no greater fulfillment than to see

God move in our lives and to be used by him to help someone else. Thank you, Chris, for your story. And thank you, God, for always being there for us and desiring to help us.

God bless,

Dr. Henry Cloud
Beverly Hills, California

CHAPTER 1

One Stoplight Town

I listened to the crunching of autumn leaves under my shoes. I walked down the back road under a canopy of trees surrounded by the Adirondack Mountains, hand in hand with my father. We were going to the family lake to meet his brothers and sisters. I couldn't have been happier. My father was my hero, and fall was my absolute favorite season. In that moment, life was grand.

We arrived at Lake Forest in the morning—RaeLynne, my eight-year-old sister; Abbeygail, who was seven; Christian, my three-year-old brother; and Jemma, who was just one. Lake Forest is close by Painted Pony Ranch, and our family has been going there for generations. My aunts and uncles greeted us with hugs and shot heckles at my father.

"Oh, nice of you to show up, baby Christian!" his older sister Betty jeered.

"Yeah. I love you too, Betty," he grinned.

I greeted my godparents with a kiss and ran straight to the water. I swam to the twelve-foot by twelve-foot floating wooden dock our uncles had made. It was covered with green lining that felt like moss under my bare feet. A group of kids were already there, playing King of the Lake, pushing each other off the dock one by one.

My father was the baby of eleven siblings, so a family outing was always an *outing*. Growing up in a large Italian-American Catholic family had its perks and its setbacks, especially because some of the relatives were legitimate gangsters. My grandpa, or "Babe" as he was known, had a terrible gambling problem. He spent his days at the Saratoga racetracks, and his habit caused devastation for the family. As a result of not wanting to grow up to be like his dad, my father was religious and despised gambling. He saw how it had destroyed his father and their family. In fact, the only time he'd take us to the races—and it was the Saratoga races only—was when the rest of the family was going. The focus then became less about the betting and more about our bonding. Thanks to my father, going to the races for me signified good, clean family time. More on that later.

When Babe and my grandmother, Champi, got divorced, the children were split up. When he was just five, my father left home to be raised by my great-grandmother, Christina Lorenzo. She was a loaded pistol. Christina was a full-blooded Italian with long light-brown hair and piercing blue eyes. She was a stern, solid-fisted woman who took over the bootlegging and gambling business for the family when my great-grandfather died. As the newspaper stories could attest, a person couldn't cross that woman and get away with it.

She raised my father with love, and my father loved her very much. When I was born, I looked nothing like my two older sisters, who were dark like my father, and my blonde hair and piercing blue eyes were a surprise. I looked like my great-grandmother. Whenever my father saw me, the "new Christina," he was reminded of the grandmother he adored.

"She was a very good lady," he told me once. "She loved me, and if it wasn't for her, my brothers and sisters and I would've starved to death. She made bad decisions, but she was a good lady. She couldn't walk down the street without someone recognizing her and coming up to her. Everyone in town respected her. She knew everyone by name. She gave everybody money too. I was the baby, so I went to church and hung around the house with her. I remember helping her hold up her mattress with money just piled underneath; I've never seen anything like it."

I felt so happy swimming at the lake in the early autumn, surrounded by my cousins, aunts, uncles, siblings—and all the delicious picnic food. Anytime we went to the lake to spend weekends with my father's family, it was guaranteed to be loud and exciting. And you could count on lots of storytelling about our past.

But the bliss faded as soon as we left the lake for our little country house atop a hill in Schuylerville, New York. As we drove, my stomach churned. I knew as soon as we stepped inside, Mother would start picking on me. And it wouldn't take long for it to get brutal and mean. As much as I tried to prepare myself on those rides home, her viciousness always surprised me.

We lived across from two huge farms that had acres and acres of corn. Our house was a fixer-upper, and my father tirelessly toiled on it when he wasn't working. He held down three jobs, but somehow, he always managed to make the best memories with us. Our backyard was in front of an old cemetery dating back to the Revolutionary War. Pine trees surrounded us for miles, and so did old tombstones.

The only other house around was across the back field. That's where Mr. Ashby lived, the old, creepy white-bearded man we loved to hate. His house was dark and spooky-looking, and we scared each other by making up stories about him stealing children or being the crypt-keeper.

"I dare you to go into his house!" one of my siblings teased.

"Go on! I'll give you a dollar!" another one chimed in.

Anytime we happened to see him, we screamed and freaked out. None of us wanted to be near Mr. Ashby. And you can be sure none of us ever were near him on purpose.

As my father pulled into our dirt driveway lined with huge pine trees, the door locks clicked open. Everyone piled out of the car, and we raced to the kitchen. Mother sometimes had supper ready when our father came home, so it was always worth checking. That day, she was holed up in their bedroom, watching the O. J. Simpson trial. She was glued to the tube during the case. She'd go on and on about a glove and how famous people get away with everything. My father went straight over to greet her, and a few moments later, we heard her laughing. Her laughter was a nice treat to hear. I don't know how he did it because she was colder than an icebox most of the time.

Why did coming home always cause me great anxiety? Because Mother and I had a downright ugly relationship. While I loved her, she appeared to hate me. She dismissed me, put me down, hit me, and hurt me, and her actions showed me just how much I was despised. My father said she never took to me—that she disliked me from the beginning, even when I was a baby. Looking back, I know it was true. According to my father, she'd leave me in the crib for hours, even if I had a dirty diaper, and then she didn't care when I got a terrible rash. When I was a toddler, she hit me whenever I was within reach, hiding the bruises with clothing. When I was around five years old, she switched from hitting me with her hands to using a metal pan or belt.

Day after day, year after year, I endured her ugliness and toxicity for no reason other than some sort of negative association she had with me—I assume because I didn't look like her or my father or any of my siblings. But her laugh could instantly give me a sense of security, short-lived as it always was, and I'd relax just a little. When she was in a good mood, it was easier to breathe. At least for the moment.

Now, after returning from the lake, I rummaged around in the kitchen, and finding no food, I ran to my room. I grabbed my little brother's Donatello Ninja Turtle and my playhouse Barbie—they were married, of course!—and crawled up to the top of my bunk bed, pulling up the metal ladder so no one could follow. I stared out the window across our backyard into the cemetery with its sea of pine trees. I loved those trees. When I played outside, I'd run as far as I could into the forest and lie under those pines. Sometimes I'd stay there until the sun started to set.

I turned my attention back to Barbie, but within just a few moments, I heard thumps and thuds coming from downstairs. Then a door slammed so loud that pictures came off the walls. Anxiety crept back into my body; my back and arms stiffened. I heard screaming voices. *That didn't take long,* I thought. Back and forth went the shouts between Mother and my father.

"I work sixty-hour weeks to put food on the table and to send our girls to the best Catholic school in the district and you can't even pay the damn tuition bill but can buy a new fur coat? Damn it, Gale!" my father screamed.

My father had found a crumpled-up late notice from our school in their bedroom. Money was often the source of the fighting.

"I deserve that fur coat. I do so much for this ungrateful family, and you can't even afford to buy me one nice thing. My parents were right!" she shouted back.

It wasn't unlike Mother to squander the money he sent home when he was away working. One time when my father returned after being away for a few months with the army, the electricity was shut off. We had been living in the dark and eating only when the nuns at school fed us. Mother didn't seem to mind a bit. She just went out to eat and bought more clothes. But this time, I could tell my father was fed up. He was exhausted from trying to convince her to be financially responsible. While I didn't understand their arguments until years later, I did understand always being hungry when my father wasn't around.

"I'm leaving!" my father shouted. "You're impossible and spoiled rotten. You better have that tuition bill paid by the time I get back!"

And with that I heard the front door slam. My heart sank. *What if he doesn't come back? Will I ever see him again? Will Mother ever be nice to me if he is gone forever?* I jumped off the top bunk and ran straight through the hall into my brother's bedroom. I stared out the window at our driveway below. My father got into the van, slammed the door, and sped off. The road made a funny noise that hurt my ears. I started crying instantly.

He left!

He left us! I couldn't believe she had really done it this time. She made him leave. As the tears fell from my face onto the carpet, I sank in front of the window. I held on to the Barbie playhouse he had gotten me for my last birthday. *Why did they always have to fight? Why couldn't they love each other like Donatello and Barbie did? Why can't Mother just do as Father asks? Why was she always angry with us kids?* My brain was littered with unanswered questions. I couldn't understand why things always had to be so hard.

Mother's voice pierced the air. "Little girl, you get down here right now!"

I immediately wiped my tears, hid my Barbie in my brother's closet, and ran downstairs. She was in the kitchen, hands on her hips and a scowl on her face. Her presence was mighty, and she was ready to give someone a whipping.

"Yes, ma'am?" I said quietly as I looked at my feet.

"You are as pathetic as your father. Crying like a baby up there. You don't think we can all hear you carrying on like a screaming banshee?" she said in a fury. I didn't say anything. I knew any response would be a wrong one, so I chose to stand still and be silent. She grabbed my face and pinched my cheeks together with her hand, forcing my head up into her gaze.

"Look at me when I'm talking to you, little girl! Who do you think you are? You want to cry? I'll give you something to cry about." She stormed off to her bedroom and came back with one of my father's belts in hand. "Pull your pants down right now!" she yelled.

I started crying and held my pink elastic britches up so tight that I gave myself a wedgie. I hooted and hollered as she whipped me from end to end. She tried to take my pants off herself, but that proved more trying than she had anticipated. She gave up and just hit me wherever she could. When she was finished, I was confused and exhausted. I looked up to see my brother and sisters huddled around with fearful faces just a few feet from us.

"Let this be a lesson to all of you. If you want to act like a spoiled brat, I'll make sure you are treated like a spoiled brat with your father's belt! Do you hear me? I don't want to see any of you crying like little babies, or I'll give you something to cry about!" she proclaimed.

Eyes swollen, nose running, body bruised. All I wanted was my father. He had just left, and I didn't know when he was going to come home again. I didn't know if he would ever come back. I was sent straight to my room after my beating, and I was grounded until further notice. As I made my way past my brother's room, I thought about sneaking in to grab my Barbie. It was too risky, so I decided to rescue her in the night when everyone was sleeping. I finally fell asleep, dreaming wild dreams of faraway places and dashing young princes who swooned over me. I was safe in my dreams. I was free to run wild beneath the pines.

A few days later at my school, St. Clement's Catholic Elementary, I was sitting at my desk when the nun teaching the class called on me to read off the chalkboard. Stunned, I lowered my head and mumbled letters that I recognized. Chatter among all the students was plentiful. So was the laughter.

"Now, children, not another word. Silence! Christina, are you having trouble seeing the chalkboard?" Sister Mary asked. I didn't understand what she meant because everything had always been blurry to me. Trees, clouds, letters, and anything far away or too close-up had always been moving in twos and threes, wobbling about in front of me.

"Yes, ma'am," I said, unsure of myself.

"Grab your things and move here," she said as she pointed to the desk next to hers.

Oh, no! Not the *bad desk*. I don't want to sit at the bad desk! What did I do wrong? As I made my way up to the bad desk, my classmates made snickering noises. I placed my books on my new desk, and I hurried to sit and be quiet to keep from disrupting the class any further.

"Now, Christina, try to read the sentence again," Sister Mary ordered.

Afraid I was going to get in more trouble, I quickly made a try at the sentence now that I could see a little better.

"Ttttt—hhh–sss pee-mm-ma-ma-kkk-aann gg-rrr-oooo-sss on a vvvv-nnnn." I sounded out each letter.

"Who would like to give this another try?" Sister Mary asked the class. My classmates shot up their hands faster than lightning. "Yes, you. Tiffany."

Tiffany quickly stood up next to her desk. Her hands smoothed out the creases in her jumper, and she began to read. "The. Apple. Is. Red," she said with little interference.

"Very good, Tiffany! You may be seated now," Sister Mary said with great delight. I felt so much shame. I kept my head down for the remainder of the day. I even kept my head down during Mass, which I usually enjoyed very much. The pretty glass and big echoes as the priest spoke his funny language were calming to me. There was so much quiet in that big cathedral. So much peace.

As we were leaving to get on the bus to go home, Sister Mary pulled me aside and put a letter in my backpack addressed to my parents. *Oh no, this is not good. What did I do wrong?* Why did she make me sit at the bad desk and why was she giving me a note to take home? I was going to be in so much trouble. I would be dead if Mother read this letter. If my father were home and he read it first, then I had hope. I wondered why he wasn't home yet from the fight they'd had a few days back. Was he working a job, and that's why he wasn't home yet? I prayed in my heart, "Dear our Father in heaven, please let my father be home today and read the letter before Mother does. I promise to listen during Mass every day if you will just let him be home when I get off the bus. And I'll give my sisters my dessert at dinner. Amen."

As I got on the bus, my two older sisters were already sitting next to each other near the back. I sat close to the front to be sure I was far enough away from them to ward off any questions about the letter. We got off the bus and began our mile trek up the very steep hill in the deep snow to our house. The hill was lined with quaint country houses from the bottom to the middle. RaeLynne and Abbeygail led the way.

It was full-blown winter, so the climb was a bit more trying than usual. It was crystal clear outside. The scent of pine trees filled the air, making everything smell like Christmas. It was colder than cold, and a light snow was blowing. It was still truly magical the way everything was covered in glistening white. I distinctly remember the vivid, crisp white all around. All three of us in our snow clothes were quite the sight! I was wearing my baby pink snowsuit, the kind like the kids wear in *A Christmas Story*. It was so big and thick that I couldn't put my arms all the way down. I looked like a miniature sumo wrestler. Then suddenly, I had to go to the bathroom. I hollered at RaeLynne, "I have to pee!"

She stopped as she turned around to face me, gripping her backpack on both straps. "Well you can't pee out here. You're gonna have to hold it till we get home."

"But I really need to go. I can't hold it. I have to go!"

She and Abbeygail just kept chirping and walking and paid no attention to my complaining. Just as the last houses on the sidewalk were coming up, I sat down in front of someone's house. I just couldn't help it. It hurt so bad that I had to go. I started crying as snow turned my dry clothes wet. Right there on the snow-covered lawn, a sharp yellow color bled around me. My sisters were well ahead of me, and they probably didn't think to look back because I was usually quiet.

I sat there crying for a good while in the yellow snow before a woman came over from her front porch and picked me up. She was wearing an apron high on her waist that was covered in flour. Her hair was in a high bun, and she was wearing her house shoes. Her feet must've been cold. I didn't know her from Adam, but she knew us kids and said her name was Mrs. Lark. She called my father right away. She took off my wet clothes and gave me dry ones, and then she made me some hot chocolate. She was so nice and comforting. I was delighted to have peed on her front lawn.

I was still at Mrs. Lark's house a few hours later when the prayer I said at school was answered. My father knocked on the glass front door, and I answered with great joy. If I had known wetting myself would bring my father when I needed him, I would have probably wet my pants more often. I hugged his neck as the snow from his big boots made the floor below me wet. He apologized profusely to Mrs. Lark. I told him not to worry. She gave me hot chocolate and colored in my coloring books with me. Mrs. Lark graciously calmed my father, and we were on our way home. It wasn't until we got in the van that I remembered the dreadful letter Sister Mary had put in my backpack. Grief swarmed over me as I anticipated what it said. But that would have to wait. My father was angry about the yard.

"What would possess you to use the bathroom while you were wearing your snowsuit and sitting in someone's front yard?" he shouted.

"I'm sorry, Father. I couldn't hold it. I told RaeLynne, but I just couldn't wait. I had to go. And before I could keep holding it, it just came out," I cried.

"Well, young lady, you had your mother and me worried sick. You are so lucky that nice woman found you! Do you know what could have happened to you? Don't you ever pull a stunt like that again, do you hear me?"

I shook my head yes as I started crying again. "I'm really sorry, Father. I love you." He looked over at me as his stern expression turned into one of compassion.

"I love you too, honey. That's why I don't want you to leave your sisters while you're walking home from school ever again. Do you hear me?" I nodded and got up out of my seat and hugged his arm as he drove home.

But the warm, loved feeling wouldn't last. As I walked over the welcome mat and into our doorway, Mother was standing in the hallway. She looked furious.

"How could you be so stupid?"

There was only silence from me and my father.

"You're always looking for attention. Just begging to get into trouble. You could've waited until you got home to go pee.

You're not fooling me, little girl. I ought to smack your butt so hard you won't be able to sit down for a week. You're making this family look like a bunch of fools!"

As she continued her rant, my father walked past her calmly into their bedroom. I stood like a deer in the headlights. I was sure any movement would infuriate her further. She followed my father as he brushed past her. I felt relieved as they closed the door behind them. I went straight into the kitchen to see if any food was lying around. RaeLynne and Abbeygail were playing *Hungry Hungry Hippos* in the TV room. After I grabbed a half-eaten Little Debbie oatmeal creme pie—Mother's favorite treat—off the counter, I sat next to them as they played.

As I relaxed and let the warmth of the kitchen cover me, I suddenly realized I'd placed my backpack on the floor by the front door. Thank goodness I could see it from where I was sitting, and I rushed to put it in my room. The rule was to never leave any of our things downstairs. I couldn't afford to break any more rules. If we left anything downstairs—shoes, snow boots, book bags, toys—Mother would become angry. And if she got angry enough, there'd be a beating too. Even my dad knew the drill. If he noticed we had left something, he'd warn, "Go pick that up before your mother sees it." That was all he had to say.

After I dropped off my backpack, I strolled into Christian's room to play. Even though he was younger, he was my very best friend. We'd play with his Ninja Turtle toys, pretend to be Mighty Morphin Power Rangers, or make colorful designs with our Lite-Brite. Lite-Brite was my favorite toy because I loved to plug the multicolored plastic pegs into the board and watch them light up. I could make anything I wanted—balloons, happy faces, stick figures of my family. Left to ourselves, Christian and I would play for hours and not bother a soul. We were good like that.

That afternoon when we were in his room, I jumped at the sound of my father calling out, "Christina, come down here please!"

I hurried downstairs, shuffled past my two sisters, and met him in the kitchen. "Yes, sir?"

"Did Sister Mary give you a letter to give to me this afternoon?"

Oh no. The letter. I had all but forgotten this letter yet again.

"Yes, sir. It's in my backpack upstairs." I anxiously played with the hem of my shirt.

"Please go upstairs and fetch me that letter, young lady," he said with a fixed brow.

I whizzed upstairs and grabbed my backpack. I rushed back into the kitchen. I placed the entire backpack at my father's feet and waited patiently for him to give another command. *How did he know I had a letter in my backpack? Who told him? Did they call him from school? That can't be good. Did RaeLynne or Abbeygail know and tattle on me?* I was so uncertain that I shuddered. I looked around for Mother. Was she about to come out of the room and spank me? Oh, boy, I was in a heap of trouble!

My mind raced as my father unzipped my backpack.

He reached his hand inside to grab the letter. He used his pocketknife to open it up and pulled out the neatly folded note. He started reading. I stared at his face, trying to decipher his thoughts. Did Sister Mary tell him she moved me to the bad desk? Why did she even put me there to begin with? Did she tell him I didn't do any of my homework correctly or that I didn't read the sentence on the chalkboard right? His face was concerned as he lowered the letter from his view.

"Christina, come here please," he asked. I walked toward him, shaking. "I want you to look out the kitchen window and tell me what you see. How many trees are by the sandbox I built for you kids?"

Staring out the window, all I could see was a bunch of blurry pine trees with white all over them and a sea of white snow covering the ground. I wasn't sure what to say. What was the right answer? I couldn't tell if there were two pine trees or four. They just all blurred together. I chose the number four. It seemed like a good number, plus I could say that number well. "Four, Father. There are four pine trees by our sandbox," I said convincingly.

"You are not going to school tomorrow, young lady. I'm taking you straight to the eye doctor," he said.

"Eye doctor? What is an eye doctor? Am I going to have to get another shot? What is he going to do to my eyes? I don't want to go, Father. What did I do wrong?" I pleaded with fear.

"Christina-beana," he said with a soft reassurance, "you need glasses."

Glasses! That's why I couldn't see the chalkboard or the

two pine trees that blurred into four. Then Mother opened their bedroom door.

"Christian, what did the school say about her this time? Does she need me to tear her hide from end to end?" A smirk of satisfaction was on her face.

"No, Gale," my father said flatly. "She's blind. We must get her glasses immediately. I'll take her first thing in the morning before work. That's why she isn't doing well in school. Sister Mary noticed it today and moved her close to her desk so she can see better. She didn't do anything wrong." He turned to me. "We'll take care of this, won't we, Christina?"

I nodded as I thought about how the bad desk wasn't bad for me, as I didn't do anything wrong after all. That was a relief! I didn't know what having glasses meant exactly, but I was sure glad that Mother didn't have a reason to whip me with my father around. The next morning, I went to the eye doctor with my father. A few days later, I would see the chalkboard for the very first time.

> The LORD sets prisoners free,
> the LORD gives sight to the blind,
> the LORD lifts up those who are bowed down.
> *Psalm 146:7–8*

CHAPTER 2

Saratoga Race Course

If my father was home, my little brother and I were with him. It didn't matter what he was doing or where he was going. We signed up for every activity and every trip. We called ourselves "the Three Cs," and we were inseparable. One of my favorite memories was our annual trip to the Travers Stakes, a huge race that took place at the Saratoga Race Course. Every year my entire family loaded up the coolers and folding chairs, and we made a party of the day. It was a total blast.

As I mentioned, my grandfather Babe was a horse racing gambler, and by sheer exposure, my father and his siblings became horse experts. Some of my uncles still work with horses to this day, running a brilliantly gorgeous Painted Pony horse ranch up in the Adirondack Mountains right by the family lake. While my father focused his time on religion (he was even a deacon at one point), he did make an exception to teach me about gambling when it came time for Travers Stakes.

I was around five years old when I learned about the

trifecta—a strategy that refers to picking three horses and then lining them up in first, second, and third place. They must complete the race in that order, or the bet (two dollars in my case) would be a loss.

When we got to the racetrack, my aunts and uncles would set up a spot behind the stadium seats on a huge patch of green grass. Within minutes, there'd be food and drinks and plenty of laughs. Group by group, we'd stroll over to the teller windows to place our bets on the horses.

My father, little brother, and I walked hand in hand through the halls of the old Saratoga Race Course. My father lifted me and then Christian, so we could tell the teller what horses we wanted to pick. Christian was the sweetest boy. He had a big grin and huge blue-green eyes that contrasted with his dark Italian skin and hair. We exchanged excited smiles, and we knew what the other was thinking: *Let's bet on a trifecta.* I loved the trifecta because it reminded me so much of my father and little brother. We three were my personal, unstoppable trifecta.

As my father leaned into the booth, I sat on his hip, level with the teller. She gave a smile while laughing politely. "Okay, little miss, what's your bet?"

I turned my head around, looked up at my father, and shrugged my shoulders. "Okay Christina, which horses did you want to pick?" he said as he folded open what looked to be a flimsy newspaper. His finger pointed to some names I was having trouble sounding out, so he began naming them one after the other. I called out the ones I liked the best.

"Little lady will take Sea Hero, Riley, and Bella—in that order please, Miss. Thank you." My father handed her two dollars in exchange for a little ticket. I wrapped my arms around my father's neck, kissed his cheek, and said thank you. Christian's turn was next, and he was just as excited as I was. After we placed our bets, we walked hand in hand all around the racetrack grounds. We stopped at the candy apple stand and then made our way back to the family picnic. It was such a great day at one of the oldest racetracks in the country. Someday I hope to take my family to the Travers Stakes at Saratoga Race Course. We'll keep making history and wonderful memories.

Another favorite memory was visiting Mr. Bullard's apple orchard in Schuylerville. As soon as the leaves started changing into purples and reds, I knew it was time for apples. Oh, how I loved autumn so much! The pumpkin patch, the corn mazes, and our favorite—apple picking! When we arrived at the orchard, we toppled out of the car, running around like little madmen. We knew we were about to pick apples with our very own hands. But first, we had to stop at the country store, where they handed out little wooden apple baskets to carry as we picked. The air was chilly, but we were so excited we didn't care. My father wore his dark brown leather jacket with the high collar. It had elastic wrists and was lined with a thick tan wool. He loved that leather jacket. I thought he looked so cool.

My father handed the cashier money in exchange for three baskets, and I heard his jacket make stretching noises.

My siblings and I immediately started arguing about who would get to hold the baskets. It was soon settled by Mother. RaeLynne, Abbeygail, and my father held the baskets as we ran off through beautiful apple trees in search of our first pick. It wouldn't be long before our father was carrying all three baskets full to the brim. Sometimes our cousins would come with us, and it would be a sea of Lorenzos taking over the apple orchard. Once we had the apples back home, we'd make cider and pies, and we'd munch on apples for our after-school snacks. Apples for weeks. It was wonderful.

While the racetrack was a blast and apple picking was chilly fun, my favorite childhood memory was going to the local dump.

Whenever my father came home after a long time away, he'd gather all the trash from around the yard and house and put it in the van. He'd call out, "Okay kiddos, who's going to the dump with their father?" Christian and I would run to get to the front door first. It may sound strange, but we knew that a trip to the dump meant more than throwing out old stinky trash; it meant a stop at the old wooden penny candy store to get Father's favorite paper dots and candy caramels for us kids. It also meant stopping at the local dairy farm to get the best soft serve ice cream in the state!

We hurried our little feet to the van, looking at each other with giggly grins. After we dropped off the trash, our father drove down the old country roads of upstate New York. We danced and jumped around in the back seat as he sang old rock songs.

We always knew when the dairy farm was coming because there was a huge bend in the road lined with pine trees. When the pine trees stopped, there was a huge green pasture that seemed to appear out of nowhere. As the tires crunched over the gravel, my excitement grew. "The Three Cs have made it!" Father said, wide-eyed and smiling. Christian and I ran straight to the line that was always long in front of the counter.

It was an outside-only ice cream parlor. You ordered at the window, and then a few minutes later, delicious homemade soft serve ice cream dipped in chocolate came right to you. It was like magic.

After we finished our cones, we walked behind the parlor to the picnic tables just across the way atop a hill and sat looking at the endless miles of green grass and dairy cows.

The Three Cs had all kinds of traditions that no one knew about except us.

> Love each other with genuine affection,
> and take delight in honoring each other.
> *Romans 12:10 NLT*

CHAPTER 3

"Laundry Lady, Laundry Lady"

It was weeks after our trip to the dump when I had one of my worst nosebleeds. It happened after school. I remember running into the kitchen to find Mother, and I tripped on some marbles from the *Hungry Hungry Hippos* game. Immediately, my nose bled—onto my clothes and the floor in the hallway. I panicked. Covering my nose, I tried to keep from making an even bigger mess. I'd already been in trouble for blood on the carpet once before.

From the time I could remember, all it took to give me a bloody nose was a quick flick of the knuckle or a spill to the ground. I remember several occasions at school when I'd be sitting at my desk, and out of the blue my nose would start bleeding. It was a constant struggle.

Using my shirt to hold my nose, my six-year-old self was

at a loss to know how to make it stop bleeding. My father was usually around to rescue me from this sort of thing. He'd scoop me up and hold me so I'd lie flat in his arms. He'd tilt my head back while holding my nose with a cotton cloth or whatever was nearby.

"How are we going to get this nose of yours to ever stop bleeding, Christina-beana? Every time I come home, you've got another bloody nose. I've never seen anything like it!"

He gave me my medicine—two pills and a nose spray. I remember taking that medicine every day for what seemed like forever.

Another time, I was playing with Christian and we were running back and forth in the hallway downstairs by the kitchen, teasing each other.

"Na-na-na waspy man gotta save me from the bees," I said, giggling and sped past him.

"I'm gonna get you with my lion!" he jeered as he held his lion by the tail, spinning it over his head. I turned, and he was coming straight for me.

Crash.

We hit head on. Within a millisecond, my nose started bleeding like a fire hydrant had exploded. There was red everywhere. It was all over my little brother. All over me. I'll never forget my father's face as he saw the carnage. He ran like lightning to us. He scooped both of us up and tried to figure out who was bleeding from where. When he discovered that all of the blood was from my nose, he held me in his arms for hours. He stripped us of our soiled clothes and took baby wipes to our faces. He told us gently, "This is why we don't run in the house. I have no doubt you two learned your lesson."

As I lay in his arms in just my Care Bear underwear, I looked down to see my little brother holding our father's hand in nothing but his Elmo Pull-Ups. He could steal your heart with just one glance. Seeing his sad, teary eyes made me so upset.

But this time, as I stood in the kitchen, my father wasn't around, and six-year-old me wasn't sure what to do to stop the bleeding. He had been gone for a few days now with the army, and I didn't know when he was coming back.

I was afraid I wouldn't be able to stop my nose from bleeding and I'd ruin Mother's carpet. So, I lay on the floor in the hallway, holding my nose with my school shirt. All I'd wanted to do was find Mother so I could read some sentences I had learned at school. She was very angry that I couldn't read yet, and she'd make fun of me in front of my brothers and sisters. I thought that reading the sentences I had learned that day would make her happy.

My older sister walked past me and stopped. "What are you doing lying on the carpet?" she asked.

"I've got another bloody nose, and I'm waiting for it to stop before I stand back up. See—there by my backpack," I replied as I pointed to the bloodstain.

"Has Mom seen this? Quick. Help me grab some rags and soap. We can clean it up, I think." RaeLynne whizzed into the bathroom and pulled the cleaner from underneath the sink.

"Go grab me that ripped-up washcloth. We'll use that," she said, pointing to the dirty laundry pile in front of the washer.

As she cleaned up the blood from the carpet, I stood before her in amazement. She was nine—exactly three years older than me. We share the same birthday, which I hated until I was in my twenties. I thought RaeLynne was the coolest girl. She was popular in school and always came home with good grades and stickers. As I stared at her while she cleaned up my bloody mess, my heart was filled with new understanding. She was helping me because she didn't want Mother to give me another spanking. She was helping me because she wanted to protect me. This was the only way she could.

At that moment I didn't say anything, but I knew she loved me.

As quickly as we could, we got rid of all the evidence of my accident. She stripped me bare, put all my clothes in the washer, and told me to put on different clothes. I grabbed her hand, squeezed it as a show of thanks, and ran upstairs to find clean clothes. I decided not to read to Mother that day and did my best to be invisible instead. In this instance, crisis was averted.

But just a few days later, we were all at the dinner table, Mother, RaeLynne, Abbeygail, Christian, Jemma, and me, when punishment would come fast and furious. I was holding my most prized possession, Bear, a small, cotton panda bear with big brown eyes and a tag that wouldn't come off its backside. He had been given to me at the hospital when I was born. He was part of me. We slept together every night. I couldn't sleep without him. I took him to school every day. We played on the playground and had lunch together. He even came with me to the bathroom. I did everything with Bear.

He was a tough little thing. I didn't know of any stuffed animal that could survive that many ripped limbs sewn back on. Thank goodness for my godmother; I wouldn't have had the years I did with Bear if she hadn't stitched him up every other week. He had little holes with stuffing brimming out the sides. He was patched up all over. His white coloring turned into a dirty gray, and his black coloring faded into a dull wash of a charcoal color. But Bear remained my most beloved friend.

So, there I was at the dinner table, eating dessert, when Bear fell out of my hands and into my bowl of chocolate pudding—rear end first. I pulled him out and Mother laughed and started singing, "Poopy bottom bear! Poopy bottom bear!" My siblings giggled and joined the chant. Over and over again, they repeated the same thing. I started to cry. "Please stop. Please stop making fun of Bear!" They kept going, and I was puffy-eyed and red-faced in frustration. I glanced at Mother. She looked excited.

I'll never forget that moment. It was when I saw the shift in Mother's heart from "I do not like this child" to "I do not love this child."

I was so young. But I saw her eyes and heard her voice. Up until that point, I believed she loved me but did not like me. I wasn't good at anything like my two older sisters or my younger brother. They each excelled in some way. I stood out because of my shortcomings. If I could become smart like

Abbeygail or pretty and funny like RaeLynne, then maybe Mother would like me too. But at that moment, I knew she enjoyed hurting me. In my realization, I immediately stopped crying and begging them to stop. I wiped the pudding off Bear and began to raise the spoon to take a bite for myself.

"Just what do you think you're doing, little girl?"

I looked up at her in confusion. "I'm eating my pudding?" I said tentatively.

Her face became hot with temper.

"No one said you could eat your pudding. We aren't done singing our new favorite song. Stand up. Get off your butt and stand in the doorway!" she yelled with a red-hot fury. I had seen this face of hers before and did not want to fall against the hand that came with it. I shot up out of my seat quicker than quick and made my way to the kitchen doorway, Bear in hand.

"Yes, ma'am," I muttered and lowered my head.

"We are going to finish our song, and you, little girl, are going to stand there perfectly still and listen. Do you hear me? Not a sound, or I will tan your hide. Kids, I want you to repeat after me as loud as you can." My brother and sisters grew pale and looked at me with fear.

I gripped Bear and whispered to his heart from mine, "I love you."

After Mother was finished, she told me to clean up the kitchen and to not come out until everything was sparkling. She excused my siblings from the dinner table, and they all scurried off. She went underneath the sink and pulled out a rusty old mop bucket and cleaner. She gave me the supplies and walked away, reminding me of the punishment that awaited me if I didn't do a good job.

I pushed a chair over to the sink, climbed on top, and filled the mop bucket with water. My mind raced. I had cleaned up after dinner before, so I knew how to do it the way Mother liked. But I had never mopped a floor before. I did remember seeing her clean the floor before my father came home. I did my best to copy how she did it.

After I cleaned the kitchen, I quietly made my way to my bedroom, hoping Bear wouldn't be taken away. I opened my dresser drawer, pulled out my Barbie nightie, and got ready for bed. I stared out the window at the tall pine trees. I drifted off to sleep with Bear in hand, dreaming of our great adventures and faraway places. Luckily, Mother left me alone.

The next day, I had the hardest time trying to write and to read the school assignments. I sounded out letters but just could not make words. Writing was also hard for me, although I was a better writer than reader. Because I was so behind in classwork, my teachers decided to keep my desk outside the classroom. I was given a different curriculum that included listening to "Hooked on Phonics" cassette tapes for hours. I had to wear bulky headphones that started hurting a few minutes after I put them on. I also had big Coke bottle glasses. They were the ugliest shade of pink, and my eyes looked huge behind the lenses. I hated my life.

If I thought dinner at home was the worst, lunchtime at school was a close second. I was picked on relentlessly by other kids. It didn't help that I had failed the first grade, a reality Mother kept fresh in my memory through her comments. Even trying my best, I just could not read, and I wanted to so badly. (Reading would elude me for years.) As the months passed, I looked at school as both a blessing and a curse—it was a blessing to be safe with the nuns and far away from Mother, and it was a curse because I was markedly different from other children.

One afternoon, I came home from school as happy as a little clam. I think I remember it so well because that wasn't a normal feeling for me! But on this day, I made a drawing for Mother. I was excited to give it to her because I thought by doing so, I'd get the kind of affection she gave my brother and sisters. With a big smile, I pulled my drawing out of my backpack and handed it to her.

I'd written "I luv you" at the top in giant, illegible letters with stick-figure drawings of us together standing by some flowers.

Mother pulled me into our laundry room, ripped the drawing out of my hand, bent over, and looked me square in the eyes. "You, little girl, are so stupid. Since you're too stupid to read and write, I'm going to help you learn what you are good for. Go get all the dirty clothes from this house. You're our Laundry Lady now. Laundry Lady, Laundry Lady—that's what we'll all call you."

She then summoned my siblings and demanded that they chant my new name while I stood next to a pile of laundry. I lowered my head. I felt the crushing weight of shame wash over me. I went from being the elephant in the room to the object of open ridicule and rejection. I longed to be like every-body else—to read, to write, to be liked. I had a terrible stutter, Coke bottle glasses that hurt my eyes, dyslexic tendencies, and a mind filled with Mother's crippling words.

When I wrote the word *love* incorrectly on the top of that gift for Mother and felt her rejection, something shifted deep inside my soul. From that moment on, I knew I was always going to be the outcast. The unwanted one. So, I was going to stop trying to get her to like me. As a child, you learn rejection quickly. And you learn to cope with rejection by accepting it.

That moment taught me not to give affection where it's unwanted, and Mother definitely didn't want it. It would take years for that wound to heal.

My joy is gone; grief is upon me;
my heart is sick within me.
Jeremiah 8:18 ESV

CHAPTER 4

South of the Mason-Dixon Line

It was almost summer break. Humidity crept up the nape of my neck. Upstate New York got *hot* that time of year. I came home from school and walked into complete disarray. Without warning and without so much as an explanation, Mother announced we were moving to her parents' house in St. Augustine, Florida, just across the Florida/Georgia line. It was nearly the end of fourth grade, but I wouldn't finish out the year. The bottom of my reality dropped out.

My grandmother, Maryam, and her third husband, Kipper, had moved to St. Augustine, and Mother had made several trips over the past couple of years to visit them. But never once had she mentioned moving there. I stood shell-shocked as she frantically crammed her clothes and toiletries into suitcases. She demanded that we pack our things too. Our father was away for work with the army, and all my brain could think about was when he'd be home. *Was he coming with us?* I asked Mother, but she didn't answer. All she'd say is that we were moving because she missed her mother more than she could stand. She looked like a tornado rummaging in the bedroom grabbing anything she could fit into the suitcase.

Mother and Grandmother had a close relationship in the sense that Mother did anything and everything that Grandmother asked. My nine-year-old self didn't understand what was going on until I saw Grandmother, who had come to New York to help with the move, sitting in the corner of Mother's bedroom. She peered over the packing, crossing her legs and folding her hands over her knees. Her presence took up the entire room.

"Gale, I told you this would happen. Now just do as I say, and I'll make sure you and that nice man you've been talking to get more time together. He's a lawyer, right? How perfectly nice. Surely he has taken you to some nice dinners so far? I just want you to be happy, Gale. Don't you know that?"

Her voice was a mixture of softness and malevolence, oozing off the tip of her tongue like honey. She had a way with words and a presence that was undeniable. It was like this invisible cloak was wrapped around Mother—a cloak made up of fear and obedience. I knew how it felt.

Grandmother was a sixties flower child. She wore a long tan skirt and a white cotton eyelet crop top with no bra. Her eyes were a cold blue. Her stringy white hair, which she purposely made messy, came just below her shoulders. She wore turquoise knuckle rings, a silver pendant that sat perfectly in the vee of her crop top, several silver bracelets on her right arm, and black boots that tied up to her ankles. Her face was weathered like leather, and she had crinkles around her eyes and mouth from years of smoking. She had a pointed nose and a mole just above her upper lip.

She terrified me.

I dashed past Mother's bedroom and into the kitchen. My two older sisters were eating snacks at the table. I sat down next to RaeLynne and asked her what was going on. She shrugged her shoulders and said, "Whatever Grandmother wants." She returned quickly to her snack.

Packing went on all night. We could take only what would fit into our bags. Mother made us leave behind all of our stuffed animals, toys, beds, furniture, and everything else. We each buried one or two trinkets deep in the bottom of our bags. But that was it.

The next morning, we filled two station wagons with cats, clothes, food, and all the kids, which by now totaled eight: RaeLynne, Abbeygail, Christian, Jemma, Carolina, Noah, Brinly, and me.

Grandmother was driving one car, and Mother was driving the other.

"I want to sit up front!" RaeLynne shouted. "I'm the oldest." She looked desperately into Mother's eyes.

"Abbeygail gets the front seat. I need you in the middle to help with the babies," Mother retorted. RaeLynne pouted as she climbed into the middle seat, whispering contempt under her breath.

The nineties station wagons had three rows. The third row faced backward. Every one of us hated the third row. It made us carsick. When you added in being next to the cats that peed and pooped in their travel boxes, being back there was downright miserable.

"Laundry Lady," Mother snarled, "I want you to sit in the very back with the cats."

"Yes, ma'am," I said as I lowered my head.

Without distractions, it was a twenty-four-hour drive from New York to Florida. It would take *us* more than two days.

Grandmother loved her cats more than anything, which is probably why Mother did too. In my eyes, they treated them better than us. Grandmother's cats got the star treatment, and at any point in time, there were four to seven furry friends roaming her big house. They had their own beds and jeweled collars. They even had special ceramic bowls with their names on them.

The only thing Grandmother spent more money on than her cats was her antiques. When she lived in New York, her house was an old Victorian mansion. It was simply gorgeous. She decorated the entire house—every room—with expensive antiques. Her parlor was her most prized room, and we were forbidden to even step foot in there. When we came over, we weren't allowed to play or run or do anything but sit on the floor in the den and watch whatever they had on TV.

My step-grandfather was at the bidding of Grandmother. He had his own business as a carpenter and was much nicer to us kids when she wasn't around, although he never really said much. He let us watch *The Last of the Mohicans* or *Walker, Texas Ranger* every time we came over. *The Last of the Mohicans* is still my favorite movie today. We watched that movie and those TV episodes anytime we were there, which wasn't very often. And if we left the den—if we so much as got near anything in her house—Grandmother would ban us from coming over for a while. It didn't take a genius to realize Grandmother didn't like kids much.

Driving down Interstate 95 with eight children was a scene to behold. Mother, true to her fashion, rationed small portions of Mama Tish's ice cups and peanut butter sandwiches to stop rumbling tummies and attempts to steal food from her bag when she wasn't looking. Woe to any child who got caught riffling through Mother's purse out of hunger!

When we arrived at our home in St. Augustine, Florida, it was hotter than a pepper patch in mid-July—much hotter than upstate New York. We had driven the entire 1,150 miles with ten people and no air-conditioning. I was sure one of us was going to die during our two-day trip.

I climbed out of the station wagon and stood on southern ground for the first time. I realized in that moment that life under this sun was going to be quite different.

Florida was stunningly beautiful. Right away, I noticed the flowers, the palm trees, and the giant oak trees covered in Spanish moss. On my new front lawn stood an oak tree with branches so big you could sit on them. The tree reminded me of the dazzling tall pines I loved in upstate New York. I ran straight for the oak and climbed up. I sat right in the middle of all its glory. The view was spectacular—for about fifteen seconds. That's all it took before Mother screamed like a banshee.

"You stupid girl, get your butt off that tree and unload this car! Who do you think you are?"

Our new home was a duplex that gave off a musty Southern charm, if there is such a thing. It was the ugliest rose pink, and the side of the house paralleled a dusty alleyway surrounded by pecan trees. Ours was the third house on a street with cracked, uneven sidewalks dotted with trees that were covered with Spanish moss. The rusty screened-in porch was peeling from the bottom up, and cat bowls littered every square inch of it. Even from the outside, it smelled of mildew, but I didn't say a peep. I knew the house had once belonged to Grandmother before she moved to a better place on the Bayfront, and Mother looked at living here as a gift.

Our part was the bottom half of the duplex, while Mother's younger stepbrother, my uncle, occupied the top half. As soon as I walked through the door, I noticed filth everywhere. The few pieces of random furniture and the walls were moldy and covered in cat hair. It would take hours to make the place even slightly presentable. I was considered the hired help, and as sure as the sun rises and sets, I would be the one charged with making the filth go away.

After we unloaded the car, Mother ordered me to start cleaning the floors, bathrooms, and kitchen. And so it began.

A group of neighborhood kids had already taken a keen interest in us, and my siblings were gunning to make an introduction. Mother told them to go ahead and play. But not me. I watched out the dingy window as they played manhunt that evening. They'd play with those kids almost every evening after school while we lived there. Every now and then, I got to join.

A week or so later, we started at our new schools. RaeLynne and Abbeygail were in the middle school, which was a few miles away, so they rode the bus. The rest of us—except for Brinly who was still in preschool—attended the elementary school just a few blocks away, and we all walked together. We woke up the babies at 6 a.m. I got them dressed, got myself dressed, and then hit the sidewalk at 7 a.m.

At the student crosswalk, we met the crossing guard, Mr. John, who was the sweetest soul. Every morning and every afternoon, he'd smile and say lovely things like, "Have a great day at school!" and "You kids walk safe." (He's still a crossing guard for the elementary school to this day!)

We walked through the school doors and into a sea of kids. Since I was the oldest, I asked the first woman I saw if she would help us get to our classes. She helped, and we settled in to our new reality. At the end of the day, we went to the after-school care program called REC (recreation, education, community) where we met Coach Troy. He had games and snacks, and we took to him instantly. We loved after-school time and hung out with about thirty other kids. When my siblings and I were hungry, which was all the time, Coach always gave us extra snacks, sneaking them to us so the other kids wouldn't see. He made us feel special—and we loved it.

When the REC time was over, Coach helped me gather up my siblings and our things and walked us to the edge of the field. He helped us get across the street and watched as we headed home. My school was a huge change from what we were all used to. But with my father still not in Florida, it was a relief to have strangers be so kind to me.

While the adults were great, I was singled out in classes. I still wore those gross thick pink glasses and didn't have nice clothes. I was shy and awkward and didn't talk much. So, I got the "new girl" treatment from other kids. It was hard going to a new school—with new people and no support from home— but I managed. We all did. Because we had to.

At home, my siblings and I mostly fended for ourselves. Mother was gone all hours of the night. When she was home, my life was consumed with chores and being locked out on the back porch doing laundry.

My shy disposition made it difficult for me to make friends. At home, the saying "children should be seen and not heard" was a genuine demand. In Florida, I didn't have my sea of pine trees to escape to, and I was outgrowing Bear. I needed to find something to help soothe my anxious mind. RaeLynne had just started singing in school and had a tape recorder.

It was her new prized possession. She would lie on our bedroom floor, wait for her favorite songs to play on the radio, and then press the record button. Her cassette tapes were my favorite. She sang everywhere in the house. I loved listening to her sing. I thought maybe I could sing too!

When the coast was clear, I hummed quietly to myself, afraid to be too loud. I decided to patiently wait for my chance when no one was around so I could sing out loud.

> They sing to the music of timbrel and lyre;
> they make merry to the sound of the pipe.
> *Job 21:12*

CHAPTER 5

"Good-bye, Father"

Even after weeks at our new house, we all still slept on the floor. We had no furniture, just a few sleeping bags, which we argued over constantly. It was hard to cook anything in our tiny kitchenette. The mini-fridge was filled with the ten-cent burgers McDonald's sold on Wednesdays. That was our week's supply of food. My father was still missing in action, and I was an emotional wreck. Where was he? What had she done to him? Why would he stay away this long? What about his promise to never leave us?

These thoughts ran in circles in my mind as I did my after-school chores. When Mother was in a good mood and I did all my chores the right way, I would muster up the courage to ask if I could call Father on the pay phone (there was one around the corner from our house). Mother said we couldn't afford a landline, so asking her was my only choice. She often answered my request by giving me another chore to do.

Late in the night after putting the kids to bed, I climbed

out my second-story window from my bedroom, stretched out on the slanted roof, and stared into the blazing sea of stars. The shingles were like sandpaper on my skin, but I needed solitude from the world. As I rested, a gentle breeze brushed over my body. I was mentally taken back to the spectacular pines I dreamed under as a little girl. As I lay under the night sky, there was peace.

It gradually dawned on me that this would be the perfect place to sing—away from the world. "Un-Break My Heart" was the first song I ever learned. With all the sorrow my heart carried, I sang that song with as much soul as Toni Braxton herself.

Singing the blues on my rooftop in Florida proved to be as peaceful as dreaming under the glorious sea of pine trees in New York. I set out to learn all the gospel songs we sang in church on Wednesday nights. Mother had made an acquaintance we called Mrs. Cindy, and she took us to church every week. Mrs. Cindy and her husband were pastors at the church, and they sometimes brought us to the beach across the street from their house on Vilano Road. They taught us to surf too! Mrs. Cindy was the nicest woman I had ever met. Her heart was as big as the ocean. I knew she loved us very much. Singing with her at church was glorious. Mrs. Cindy taught me all the lyrics and gave me hymnbooks to take home. I felt a healing balm of release with every riff I sang.

That night on the rooftop, I stopped singing when I heard footsteps. Curious and a little fearful, I peered over the roof to the front of the house. I gripped a post from the front balcony for balance. I saw Mother and a strange man embracing right in front of our house. They shared a kiss! In shock, I crawled off the roof and back into bed. I lay perfectly still next to my little sister and brother as my heart and mind raced. Who was this man? Why were they kissing? What was my father going to think?

The front door creaked open, and I heard Mother sneaking into her bedroom. She hadn't been home in days. Even at nine years old, I knew exactly what was happening. I didn't know what to call it, but she wasn't being faithful to my father. The man she kissed was tall, lanky, dark-skinned, and well dressed, but he certainly wasn't as handsome as my father. Even from my rooftop view, I could tell this man had an air of creepy arrogance. What did she possibly see in him? Hours later, I finally fell asleep. The next morning was the beginning of the end of our small-town family.

Knock. Knock. Knock.

We all heard the knock from the kitchen. Through the window I could see it was my father! Praise God! I was the first one to get to the door to greet him. He scooped me up and kissed my little forehead. It had been six weeks since I'd seen him, and now all was right with the world.

"Christina-Beana! How are you, baby?" my father asked with joy.

While he was speaking, he scooped up little Christian, and my younger sister Carolina grabbed onto his leg. He gave hugs and kisses to each of us. He didn't make it past the doorway.

Mother came out of her bedroom, and an arctic breeze followed. It wasn't long before my parents shut Mother's bedroom door and the screaming began. Still, it was so nice to have him home. Soon we had furniture, food in the fridge, and new shoes for school. Everything was different when our father was around. I didn't say a word about what I had seen from the rooftop.

Shortly after coming to Florida, my father opened a French bakery on Anastasia Island. He was an excellent baker and chef. Just before we left New York, he had opened a coffee shop at the bottom of the steep hill we lived on. That was one of the reasons he couldn't get to Florida sooner. He had to close his shop, sell the house, and tie up all the loose ends Mother had left when she abruptly moved us to the South. Now, in Florida, he focused on making a success of his new venture. With eight kids to feed, Father worked all the time.

Whenever we could, we accompanied him to work. We learned to make croissants, Napoleon pastries, and all kinds of decadent treats during those few months at the bakery. I was never prouder than I was at my father's bakery. I wore his oversized apron, mixing pounds of butter and sugar in the giant mixing machine.

"Okay, Beana, take these sticks of butter and put 'em in the mixer; then we'll add the eggs." Grinning from ear to ear, I stood on the chair and baked with my father. All of us helped around the bakery. RaeLynne and Abbeygail would sometimes be cashier girls, while the Three Cs baked in the back. No matter how small or young we were, Father found a job for each of us.

About six months after joining us in Florida, we had all settled into a routine. One fateful day, I was, as usual, watching out the window for my father to come home from work. When I saw his car drive onto our street, I ran downstairs and flung open the front door, running toward him as fast as my little legs would carry me. He picked me up, rested me on his hip, and kissed my forehead. It wasn't but a moment later when we heard sirens down the street. Suddenly, three police cars swerved in front of us and parked abruptly. The officers jumped out of their patrol cars and rushed toward us, pistols fixed on my father.

"Sir, you are not allowed to be here at this home. Put your daughter down and walk slowly with your hands behind your head." My Italian father laughed as if he knew they had made a huge mistake.

"What do you mean I can't be here? You've got the wrong man. This is my home, and these are my children!"

By now, all my brothers and sisters were on the front porch, looking through the tattered screen. Five police officers were holding my father at gunpoint in front of that dreadful duplex. I could see our neighbors standing on their lawns, waiting to see what would happen next.

"Mr. Lorenzo, we know you've been abusing your wife. Put your daughter down, or we'll take her from you," one officer demanded.

I burst into tears. I knew they were going to take him

away, so I latched on to him, refusing to let go. My father quietly coaxed me to the ground, explaining that there was a misunderstanding. He was going to clear it up with these men. I didn't need to worry; he would be home soon.

I was crying hysterically as I let go of my father. He was handcuffed, and a police officer ordered me to go back to my house. Another officer placed him in the back of the cop car and drove away. I stood in the middle of the road, looking at my father's face as he turned around to stare back at me. There were tears in his eyes.

Words will never do justice.

When I walked back to the house, I was an absolute mess. Mother came down the stairs and summoned all of us to the kitchen. My siblings didn't say a word. We just stared at each other in complete confusion. I felt a hand grip the back of my neck. Mother squeezed her nails into my skin, pushing me into the kitchen and down to the floor in front of my siblings. She started kicking me and screaming about how I had made her look bad in front of the police by sobbing like a baby. My siblings sat at the kitchen table in silence. She then ordered me to get up and stand perfectly still with my hands by my sides.

It may seem like an easy request, but for years, Mother had beat me so badly I would flinch if the wind blew past me. I was unable to stand perfectly still before her—or anyone, for that matter. I flinched with every move she made, knowing that one of those moves was going to be a blow to my face or my stomach. I stood there, hands by my sides, and I decided I would not protect myself.

I had just been torn out of my father's arms, and I was empty inside. I was confused, angry, sad, and worn out. I became a hollow shell of a little girl. I stood before her and for the first time looked into her eyes while she bellowed out the insults.

"You dirty whore, we all know you are a filthy whore. Like a demon. You are just a dirty little demon."

I was never to look at her, never ever to look her in the eyes. She wouldn't have it. But this time, I was standing my ground. I looked into her eyes without fear, and she raised her left hand and slapped my face as hard as she could. Her triangle-shaped ring caught my eye and split it open. There was blood on my face, but I didn't move, beg, or cry out for mercy. I lifted my face after the hit and stared intently again into her eyes. She punched me to the floor. I stood up again in complete defiance, resolved not to sob or show any pain. I stood up straight again, my hands by my sides.

She took the end of a broomstick and then her belt buckle and beat me until I was limp on the floor. I didn't get up again after that. But I didn't shed one tear either.

I held on to the rage deep inside me. Everything was a swirl of confusion, of questions, of wishing my father was there. But that horrible day, the day my father was taken from me, I resolved to be everything she wasn't. I decided I was going to be loving, kind, and hardworking. A good mother, and a good person. She could do as she pleased right now, but one day I would rise above all the mean things she said about me. One day, I would grow up and be the opposite of her.

After the whipping, she demanded that my siblings gather around and chant, "Demon, demon, demon, you are nothing but a demon." They knew they had to do what she asked. And so the siblings who were present chanted as I lay on the floor, helpless and stripped of any hope that life with her would ever be anything better. I only had my conviction to become everything she said I wasn't.

As the years went on, my identity would be wrapped up in doing all the chores in the house. The names she called me evolved. They grew more hostile over time—much more hostile than "Laundry Lady." After my father was no longer there to keep me safe, the nicknames Mother found to be fitting were Demon, Slut, Whore, Stupid, and Idiot—in no particular order. I went years without ever hearing my own name. At one point, it was so bad that my brothers and sisters weren't allowed to speak to me unless she gave permission, and I wasn't to eat at the same time as they did. After supper, I would clean the kitchen, and then I would eat leftovers—that is, if I had cleaned the kitchen to Mother's specifications.

The day they took my father away from me, my world turned horribly bleak.

My father was charged with spousal abuse and thrown into the county jail. The man I had seen kissing Mother came over. There was just something about him that was dark. He had a cloud of something over him, but I kept all that to myself. I knew Mother was seeing him, and I believed he was the reason my parents broke up. But what I learned after he walked through our door that day scared me even more.

Mother came out of her bedroom dressed in a spectacular sundress that made her look angelic. She was stunning. She was perfectly tan with freshly colored blonde hair. She beamed with a glow I had never seen before. She walked over to the front door as if she was walking on clouds to introduce us to the mysterious man, Herman Hitchcock. We huddled around the stair banister by the front door. He kneeled down and pulled out what looked like a wallet from his back pocket. He opened it and revealed a shiny badge with a "St. Johns County Sheriff's Office" emblem emblazoned around a sheriff's star. He told us with pride that he was the lawyer for the sheriff's office.

"Do you know what this means, kids?"

"No, sir," my older sister blurted out. We all shook our heads in ignorance.

"This means that in this town I am in control." He held out the badge. "Want to hold it?"

No one said a word; we all just stared at him in confusion. Mother quickly shooed us to other things and told us she would be back later in the evening. She and Herman were going out to dinner.

A happy heart makes the face cheerful,
but heartache crushes the spirit.
Proverbs 15:13

CHAPTER 6

Laundry Room Miracles

Long summer nights in the sweltering southern heat called for makeshift fans out of old newspapers. I heard the constant sound of Mother's bedroom fan clicking as if it would die at any moment. When she was away, we grabbed her fan, took it into the den, and faced it toward the front door, trying different angles. We were searching for sanctuary from sweat. We took turns talking into the fan to hear our voices morph into some robotic creature, and we'd have a moment of refreshing comfort.

Not long after my father was hauled away to the county jail, Mother and Herman announced they were taking a vacation. Mother came home with a present from Herman—a shawl to wrap around her head. They were going to Turkey, and she couldn't dress like an American there.

I remember thinking how odd it was for them to go on vacation without taking us, and how weird it was that she had to wear a headscarf. We had never gone on a weeklong vacation, although our father always managed to work hard enough to pay for trips to the aquarium or weekend getaways to Martha's Vineyard. Mother was going out of the country for the first time, and it was obvious from how she pranced around that she was excited to have a man of wealth. Our father's income was modest and every dollar was stretched with eight children and a stay-at-home wife. I can only imagine the sacrifices he must have made to care for us all.

Mother and her new man never invited us kids to do anything or go anywhere. Not lunch, supper—I mean *nowhere.* This reality was such a contrast to having a father who wanted us with him everywhere he went. Now the most we ever saw of this man with the badge was at our front door when he picked Mother up or dropped her off.

When Mother told us she would be leaving for two weeks, part of me was relieved to the point of celebration. The other part of me was sad that she didn't want us to go with her.

Mother gave RaeLynne and Abbeygail instructions for watching us and told me that all my chores and the after-school rules would not change. I realized things really weren't going to be much different because in Mother's normal routine, she'd leave us for days at a time, only coming home to take a shower or get clothes. To help RaeLynne during her trip, Mother asked her stepbrother, our uncle Talmon, to check on us periodically. He lived upstairs in the studio kitchenette. A few times he'd come in through the back door, find RaeLynne, chat for a bit, and then go back upstairs. For the most part, we were totally on our own.

While Mother was away, I slacked on my laundry chores. The piles of dirty clothes had stacked up so high that it hit midway up the wall. Mother was scheduled to return in a couple of days, and the sight of three huge baskets smashed against the wall made me panic. I never managed to get to the bottom of the baskets, but I washed, dried, folded, and put away as many loads a day as I could. I could usually do about four or five.

I'd drop my book bag and hustle through the long entrance that started at the front door and ended at the kitchen back door. Our screened-in back porch was directly behind the kitchen. Rust on the window frames had chipped the paint and scattered it on the floor. A few pieces of old dirty furniture lined the back wall. There were tools, paint buckets, broken wooden chairs, and a slew of other leftover items strewn around. The smell of mildew from the fierce Florida rain was ever-present.

Our washer and dryer were isolated inside a small corridor on the back side of the house, with just enough room for one person to navigate. I reached inside the washer, catching my shirt on the rusting metal edge. It scraped my skin and made a hole in my shirt, but most of my shirts were torn so it wasn't a big deal. I had bigger things to think about.

Although the back porch wasn't inviting or pleasant in any way, I learned to cultivate a space of peace. Every time I shut the kitchen door behind me, I walked into a world of beauty. A world I had created for myself.

I could be anyone I wanted to be, and I could be loved. As I did my family's laundry, I made up songs about how they loved me and how God loved me. I thought back to the times when

Mrs. Cindy told me stories about God's love. I daydreamed of my future prince, who one day would gallantly save me from the wicked witch who chained me to this wretched dungeon. I sang songs to the air, and I turned the cramped room into a space of rest for myself. It was as if God himself came into that filthy laundry room with me—his love-drenched presence absorbing all my grief. The hours, days, and years I spent in the laundry room taught me how to dream.

Who am I?

Who do I want to be?

I was very young when I began asking these questions. Most of the answers came the night Mother whipped me after Father was taken to jail.

Who am I? I am not Mother!

Who do I want to be? I want to be someone who has a loving family.

I was convinced my desires and dreams would be reality. Someday.

Mother returned from her vacation and asked me to get her brother from upstairs because it was dinnertime. I opened the back door, walked through the laundry room, and bolted up the outside stairs on the back of the house. I flung open the door. It startled my uncle, who jerked his gaze away from his computer screen.

Leaning into the door, I announced, "Uncle Talmon, Mother told me to tell you it's time for dinner."

"It's not dinnertime! Come here, you little brat!" he said as he grinned at me. His hands moved up toward his face in claw shapes.

"Haha! No, Uncle Talmon, don't get me!" I screamed as I ran into his living room. Chasing after me, he scooped me up by my hips and spun me around. We stared into each other's faces, laughing.

"You won't get away from me, little Laundry Lady! Oh, no, you won't!" I laughed as my little feet flew beneath me. As he put me down, his shirt flew up. My feet touched the floor and I was level with his belt.

His pants were undone, and he was exposed.

My face went stone-cold, and my body was completely still.

He stared back at me, unable to speak. I had never seen a man this way before. I had never even seen my father in his underwear. He made a point to always be covered in front of us girls.

Shell-shocked but aware that this was something bad, I blurted out, "I won't tell anyone; just let me go."

In that moment, his demeanor completely changed. His face transformed from fear to evil. It was like something became unleashed. It was terrifying.

"My sister hates you. She won't care if I punish you." He released my arms and told me to pull down his shirt. I did as he asked and ran out the back door down the stairs to the laundry room. His laugh echoed in my ears.

Why did this happen? Was it my fault because he was tickling me? Did I do this to him? With that first experience of a new form of abuse, I became trapped inside the words I had heard for years. *You are ugly. Nobody loves you. You're a stupid bitch. You are crazy. This is all your fault. Your father hated you. You are too dumb to read. You're an idiot. You slut. You dirty whore.* On and on these thoughts plagued my mind.

I could hear the crunching of the pecan shells underneath his shoes and the creak of the broken screen door as he opened it. I stopped pulling laundry out of the washer. I held my breath, hoping he wouldn't walk toward the small corridor. But he did walk toward me, and I could smell him. My body shuddered in disgust. He grabbed me, one hand around my waist and one around my mouth. I kicked and screamed. I bit his hand, and I wept bitterly. Couldn't someone catch him? Couldn't someone see him hurt me? Someone should care. His laugh rang through my mind as I struggled to be free from him. I was in the fourth grade, and my tiny frame was not strong enough to stop a grown man in his twenties. I was crushed by him.

"Your mother will never believe you," he whispered into my ear, his breath hot. "It doesn't matter what I do to you. She will never be angry with me. I am her brother. You are nothing to her."

The door was open, and I could hear the laughter and chatter of my brother and sisters. I was desperate for one of them to find me. I was crying and yelling at him to stop, fighting back as hard as I could. He put his hand over my mouth in an attempt to shut me up.

"I'm almost finished. You f—king better stop moving."

As I turned my head to the side, tears ran down my cheeks. I looked out past my bedroom door and into the hallway. But no one heard me. No one came in. No one saved me. I lay hopelessly underneath the weight of evil, and I begged God to take my life.

How did I escape the reality around me? How did I maintain sanity in a world that told me daily I was worthless? How did I manage to survive the unapologetic exploitation that came for me every morning? I closed my eyes, dreamed of a faraway place, and ran away.

I drifted away every time I went out on the back porch to do laundry, every time I put my head down to sleep, every time I had the opportunity to be alone with my thoughts.

With this new predator out to hurt me, I felt even more lost. Days turned into weeks, weeks into months, months into years. For almost four years, I was raped in every corner, every closet, and every bed in our house. No one heard me. No one saw me. No one helped me. Talmon knew I was the outcast. And because of that, I was an easy target.

To cope, I pulled out all my hair, strand by strand. It left bald spots all around my head. This invited new torments, new nicknames, and new wounds to be healed. My hope pushed me to believe that one day, the Lord would redeem me—and my family. I was sure I would have the fairy-tale ending of Cinderella—and the redemption of Joseph from the Bible.

Months later, I was in the laundry room, not singing or dreaming like I once had done, but helplessly going about my chores. I was a hollow being. As I folded my baby brother's wrinkled T-shirt, I was paralyzed with grief. Suddenly, a presence took over the laundry room. It rendered me immobile. I listened to the silence. Then my fear slowly turned into unspeakable joy. The darkness that surrounded me inexplicably turned into bright light.

What was I seeing?

What was happening to me?

A blanket of perfect peace enveloped me. My heart burst with laughter. I looked up to the ceiling and saw nothing. But when I closed my eyes, I saw the living God arrayed in all his glory. Love surrounded me. I began to hope again.

Hope is a fearsome thing.

It moves men to war. It compels mothers to pray without ceasing. It convinces women to stand firm in the face of absent love. As this transcendent hope welled up in me, I saw the beauty of life. It was as if God reached into my body, pulled out my beating heart, and placed it underneath the heavenly lid of a glass jar. This supernatural experience is the moment I grasped the awakening power of hope.

I have cleaved to it ever since.

A bruised reed he will not break,
and a smoldering wick he will not snuff out.
In faithfulness he will bring forth justice.
Isaiah 42:3

CHAPTER 7

Locked Away

I looked up at a frazzled teacher.

"Young lady, answer the question!" barked Mrs. Stone.

I had lost myself in a daydream. I didn't hear her question, and I was unable to answer. Instead, I looked at the floor. I didn't care about anything. The abuse had taken its toll, and I was no longer participating in much. I was mentally and physical exhausted. I was so skinny and so broken that the only reason I had survived up until this point was Jesus. There was no other explanation.

In exchange for my silence, the teacher revoked my recess privilege for the day. As I sat on the concrete steps by the entrance to the playground, I tightened my finger around a small section of my hair. With a quick jerk, the hair was a clump in my hand. The brief pinch on my scalp brought me back to reality. The other kids were playing, but I had nothing. Because of my uncle's abuse, I had subconsciously started pulling out one strand at a time. The comb-over Mother gave me did little to hide the bald patches. Hair grew back like spikes next to new bald areas. I had a new nickname at school—Spike.

At lunchtime, I waited in the cafeteria line, where a group of girls taunted me. Their insults were nothing new. I lowered my head in shame. Because the girls were holding up the line, kids started to go around us to get their lunch trays. Then out of nowhere, a pair of tennis shoes stopped parallel to mine.

"It's not nice to make fun of people. Especially those who are smaller than you. Leave her alone, okay? We don't want any trouble." The owner of the mystery shoes grabbed my hand. He ushered me in front of him and grabbed two lunch trays. He asked the lunch lady for an extra milk.

"Thank you for . . . I'm Chris," I said sheepishly as I followed him out of the lunch line.

"I know your name. Sorry those girls were mean. Just follow me and no one will bother you, all right?"

We walked out the side cafeteria door. The kids outside stared at us intently, fixated on his every step. I knew right away that this boy must be popular. He carried both trays as we walked behind the gym. He sat down on the highest concrete step outside the gym and placed our lunches side by side. I stood still for a moment, not knowing what to do. He had sun-kissed skin, blond hair, and the bluest eyes. *Who was this boy? How did he know my name? Why was he being so nice to me?*

"You can sit down now, Chris. I don't bite." He pushed my tray closer to me with a wide-eyed smile. I stared at his boyish grin and gave a little laugh as I sat down next to him.

"What's your name? Thank you again for getting my lunch. I could eat two of these."

"I'm Danny. Don't worry. Since we're friends now, no one's gonna mess with you—I promise."

I stopped chewing and lowered my sandwich to my lap. *Who was this boy?* I nodded my head in appreciation and grabbed my milk carton as I finished chewing. I didn't say another word while we ate. When we were finished, he picked up our trash and walked me back to class. Almost every day until Danny Swanson graduated from the fifth grade, he ate lunch with me. When I was with him, no one called me Spike. Danny was my only friend at school.

After three years without my father, I was resigned to the reality that I was, now and forever, the family outsider. I was slogging around this new normal, until another shock came. One afternoon, unexpectedly, Mother came home to tell us she was getting married to Herman—and that she was pregnant. I was in the sixth grade, attending middle school, and while I got to see father a few times in the first months when he was in jail, after that, visitation was severed due to the allegations against him.

Social workers and policemen had been showing up at our doorstep a few times a month, and I found out later that these visits were a result of my father's tireless efforts to save his kids from all the abuse he believed was going on. My father was in and out of jail for years on various charges ranging from domestic abuse to failure to pay child support and contempt of court—all of it relating to the issues within my family.

From his jail cell, my father sent hundreds of written requests for intervention. He wrote to the St. Augustine courthouse, the state's attorney, local Department of Children and Families (DCF) officials, and even the governor. Father pleaded with anyone who would listen about the neglect and mishandling of our court case—and of us. But every time he sent a letter, he was directed to someone else, who would then send him to someone else. His efforts to save us were paralyzed. It is my understanding he was placed in contempt for calling the police to our house so much on suspicion of abuse. I was always wondering if Herman's position in the sheriff's office made it difficult for any allegations to stick.

My father desperately wanted to win back custody of his children. He wanted to prove he was innocent of the domestic abuse charge leveled by Mother. But he was shut down at every turn. Any time police showed up to investigate the abuse claims, Mother made sure she was at home, coaching me on exactly what to say when they asked me if she was hurting me. Every social worker, police officer, and DCF official came and left without ever speaking to me alone. When Mother married Herman, my father pushed for greater scrutiny. He simply wasn't going to let up.

Eventually, Mother and Herman grew tired of the questions and visits and decided to move. They pulled us out of school mid-semester, forcing me to leave what had finally become comfortable to start over at a new middle school.

This new school was totally uptown proper. Every child had designer clothes, shoes, and backpacks. Like the rest of my siblings, I wore hand-me-downs until they were bursting at the seams and unable to be mended. Forget the department stores—Goodwill was Mother's favorite place to shop for us kids.

Because of the way I dressed, I stood out like a sore thumb at my new middle school. But luckily, I wasn't as awkward-looking as in years past because my hair had finally grown long enough to hide the bald patches. I was able to be a little bit more engaging with my peers. And within my first week of school, I miraculously made two friends—Rachel and Christina. They were like sunshine.

Rachel and Christina were inseparable best friends. They ate lunch together, played at recess together, and sat next to each other on the bus. I met them at the bus stop. I immediately noticed that they were pretty and loud—and they seemed fun. They were standing there, putting on makeup and fixing each other's hair—activities I knew nothing about. I never wore makeup, and the only thing I knew to do with my hair was hide bald spots.

I was spellbound by their joyous camaraderie. I stared at them from just a few feet away as we stood in the chilly winter weather, and I noticed Christina staring back at me.

"Oh, I am so sorry. I just noticed your makeup." I dug my hands deeper into my jacket.

"Want to try my lip gloss?" Christina reached into her book bag and pulled out a lustrous pink gloss. She stretched her hand out to mine and smiled at me. "I don't have germs! It's safe." Mesmerized by her, I slowly took the lip gloss, opened the top, and applied it to my lips.

"Thank you. Does it look okay?"

Rachel beamed bright with a genuine grin. "You are really beautiful." Shocked at her compliment, I asked them if I could sit with them on the bus. They agreed, and we chirped all the way to school.

Rachel and Christina quickly became my two best friends. Before them, all I had was Bear, and my only friend had been Danny (and that had been only during lunchtime), so having girlfriends was a real treat. I never knew what it was like to talk about other girls or giggle at cute boys. Sitting with someone on the bus or meeting up at lunchtime was pure bliss to me. I opened up to them quickly. Soon I was standing on cafeteria lunch tables belting out Christina Aguilera songs as I entertained the two girls who enjoyed my singing as much as I did.

One afternoon when the three of us got off the bus, Christina invited me over to her house for a snack. I wasn't allowed to go anywhere after school, but because Mother was usually out when I got home, I figured it would be okay. But on this particular day, by sheer happenstance, Mother was driving into the apartment complex. She saw me with Rachel and Christina. As soon as I got home, she forbade me to hang out with them.

This only meant I'd have to get clever about spending time with my friends.

My new laundry room was down by the clubhouse just outside the pool area. I had to carry big baskets of clothes filled to the brim down three flights of stairs. I dragged them across the sidewalks to the noisy coin-operated machines. But there was a bonus to all that hard work: the laundry room was where my two new best friends hung out with me. They played around the complex and kept lookout. They'd sit on the washer, and we'd talk and laugh while I did my daily chore. Unfortunately, it didn't take long for Mother to find out about my visitors, and I was on the receiving end of a whupping with her belt.

Despite the pain and her meanness, the beating did little to sway me from sneaking them into the laundry room. I did, however, have to wear long-sleeved shirts to cover up some bruises.

One afternoon, Rachel met me in the laundry room. She sat on top of the dryer as I unloaded the washer. I pushed up my sleeves without a thought, and when I stood up, wet clothes in hand, Rachel's eyes were fixed on my arms. I dropped the clothes. Before they hit the floor, I'd pulled down my sleeves.

"You can't tell anyone, Rachel. Mother will kill me if anyone finds out," I said with fear in my eyes.

She said nothing.

"Please, Rachel. You can't say anything. I'm fine! They don't even hurt. You know how Mother is. Okay?"

She hopped off the dryer, tears in her eyes, and hugged me. "I won't tell, Chris. I feel so bad. I'm sorry she hurts you."

Embracing her harder, I started crying too.

Rachel told Christina about what she saw. They cornered me at school and demanded I tell them everything.

So I did.

I found the greatest relief as I told my deepest pain to my close friends. These secrets were supposed to go to the grave with me. Mother escaped the constant stream of DCF workers and policemen showing up at our door to question us, but my two middle school girl friends had questions of their own, and I could answer without the fear of Mother. I spoke the truths that had made me a hollow child, and peace came over me. I released all my wounds into the open. In that moment, my body and mind began their very lengthy healing journey.

A few days later when I was bathing the little ones, Mother was on the back porch smoking her clove cigarettes and drinking red wine with Herman. My little sister Carolina, who at this time was eight, had finished doing the dishes. She walked into our bedroom and sat on our bed, preparing to read a book. She could read so well. I enjoyed watching her speed through all the books she got from school. After tucking in the babies, I took a moment to sit with her while she opened her book.

Suddenly, we heard Herman scream out, "Carolina Lorenzo! You get your tiny butt in here right now!"

The babies woke up. Slamming the book shut in fear, Carolina ran to the kitchen. I stayed in our bedroom but leaned against the crack in the door so I could see what he was going to do. He grabbed her by the neck and pushed her head in the sink.

"You see this trash in the sink? You idiot, who taught you how to clean?" He picked up each plate she had just washed and smashed it on the kitchen floor at her feet. Plate after plate shattered as she stood there in silent tears. He just laughed as she cried. After the fifth plate, I realized she had no shoes on.

I ran to the kitchen and stood in front of my little sister, yelling frantically. "Are you *crazy*? She has no shoes on, look! Her feet are bleeding. What is wrong with you?"

I was so very angry. I couldn't bear to see Herman or Mother abuse my siblings. I was used to it, had even grown comfortable being the scapegoat, but I wasn't going to stand by watching them inflict pain on the other kids.

It only took the time for the word *you* to escape my mouth before he grabbed me by the throat. He lifted me off my feet into the air, choking me. He took me out of the kitchen into the hallway and slammed my body against the wall. Cursing with words that until that point were unfamiliar, he slammed my body against the wall again and again until I went limp. As I slid down the wall in slow motion, I could hear Mother laugh in excitement. I was barely conscious, so I thought maybe I had lost my mind.

Then as Herman released me, she walked over to where I lay.

"That'll teach you to keep your filthy mouth shut!"

After I was beaten, I pushed myself to stand. Herman and Mother ordered me to clean the broken dishes—in bare feet.

That night after we were all in our bunk beds, I plotted with Carolina, Noah, and Brinly to run away. I opened our window to judge the distance to the ground below, but I knew it was too far down. We dreamed of getting out as we stared out into the sea of cars in the parking lot and on the buzzing highway nearby. I held all three of them closely, apologizing for not being able to protect them, promising not to let anyone ever hurt them again. I knew I couldn't keep that promise. With tears in my eyes, I rocked each of them to sleep, begging God to save us.

A few days later, my siblings were chatting about how Mother said our uncle was coming to stay with us. Fear crippled me. Nightmares were common, but when I heard he might be staying with us, I began having night terrors. I was determined not to let my uncle hurt me or anyone else ever again. I contemplated for days whether to tell Mother what he had done to me. I finally decided I had to let her know, and the day I planned to tell her, I had crippling anxiety. I walked on pins and needles all day at school. I didn't eat lunch. In our house, lunch was usually the only regular meal, so forfeiting it was sheer madness. I'd tell her as soon as I got home from school.

I walked in the house and noticed Herman wasn't there yet, thank goodness. I asked Mother if I could talk to her. She was perplexed. I had never asked to speak to her, let alone with no one else around. I led Mother into our bedroom and closed the door behind her. I sat on the edge of the lower bunk bed facing the window. I was sweating, gripping my clammy hands and unable to speak for fear that she would literally kill me. I stuttered for several minutes with words that didn't even make sense. She lost her patience, and with coiled lips she gave me an ultimatum: "I don't have time for these games, little girl. You have thirty seconds to spit it out before I get the Palmolive."

Oh no. Please, Jesus, not the green Palmolive! Mother would make us sit in a chair, tilt our heads back, and pour green Palmolive in our mouth. She forced us to leave our mouths open and our heads tilted back as the soap burned through our tongues. Most of us endured this punishment at one time or another. If we moved or cried or breathed the wrong way, we'd end up swallowing an entire mouthful of dish soap. It was by far one of the worst punishments she gave us. I hated it, and she knew it, so I quickly gathered my thoughts.

I lowered my head and said, "Talmon touched me."

Silence.

"What did you just say, young lady?"

I told her he had started abusing me when I was nine and that it went on until we moved a few months back. I had never seen Mother so incensed.

"You lying whore! This is what you wanted to say to me? You stupid slut." Her voice was raging with fire. She peered at me with dark eyes, and her voice became a violent whisper. "You. Stupid. Little. Slut."

She screamed nonsense as she grabbed me by the back of my neck and forced me toward the door. She dug her nails into my neck, and I wept. There I was, in the hallway on my knees. My other siblings watched as Mother beat me with her belt. She hurt me so badly that I couldn't sit down for more than a week without flinching. After Mother was done punishing me, she grounded me to my room, took away my next three meals, and told me I was only allowed to use the bathroom if Abbeygail said I could. I regretted ever telling her anything about her brother and wished I had kept my mouth shut. When Herman arrived, Mother pulled him into her bedroom. They talked for several hours before coming out. She left without saying a word.

Where was she going? What had I just done? I was consumed with fear.

The next morning, I woke up and got my little brother and sisters dressed, fed, and ready for school. Walking them to the bus stop, I had the worst feeling deep in my belly. Unbeknownst to me, the night before Mother had driven over to Grandmother's house to have a family discussion. Talmon was staying with them. And after RaeLynne and Herman had a fight and he subsequently kicked her out of our house, she was there too. RaeLynne would be the one to tell me everything that had been said that night.

That night, Mother, Grandmother, and RaeLynne sat in Grandmother's living room across from Talmon and asked him if what I said was true. He told them it was my idea and that he was sorry.

"I knew she was a little whore," Mother said. "She probably asked for it, didn't she? Don't worry, Talmon. We will fix this, and no one will ever find out."

Mother and Grandmother devised a plan to protect Talmon from getting into trouble for raping me. Grandmother advised that it would be best to keep Talmon far away from me to avoid incurring any more "issues."

Mother and Grandmother then tasked my older sister with making sure Talmon and I were never in the same room. My sister explained to them that I would *never* go anywhere he already was. She was confused and began to cry. Even now, my heart breaks for my sister. She endured such pain. Grandmother silenced the room and demanded that no one ever speak of it again. And with that, the cover-up of Talmon's horrific sexual abuse against me began. My family chose to protect a pedophile instead of me.

Even after we moved, my father fought for justice on my behalf. He knew I was being abused, and he went to court for years. He took each denied motion to another higher court or government entity. He took our case from the Seventh Judicial Circuit Court, which denied almost every one of my father's motions starting in 1996, to the Court of Appeals, to the Supreme Court of Florida. He filed petitions, motions, briefs, and even a writ of habeas corpus in federal court in Jacksonville, Florida, on behalf of all eight of his children.

He filed letters and requests for help with the FBI, DCF, state attorney's office, St. Johns County School District, St. Augustine Police Department, and St. Johns County Sheriff's

Office. He fought to have our case reinvestigated properly for child neglect. He did all this while under extreme duress and even after having a stroke!

My father was no angel. He had made mistakes that put his kids in harm's way, but once he realized the full extent of what Mother was capable of, he tried to save us. He tried for years and years.

By this time, I was a teenager, and I wondered if everyone in St. Augustine knew we were being abused and neglected. I wondered why no one did anything about it. I also wondered if Herman's position caused the authorities to turn a blind eye to the situation in our home. Perhaps the authorities didn't believe abuse could happen in the home of a man of his standing. Or was it due to the political lashing Herman could inflict? He was a powerful man in the community—a badge-carrying lawyer for the sheriff's office. But he was only one man.

The only person who ever tried to help me was my father. As his prison term wore on, he continued to send letters, even trying congressmen, state representatives, and Governor Jeb Bush, begging for someone to look into our case and save us. As with his first efforts, the response letters he received back always sent him to another governing body or office. States like Florida that uphold the silent "mother law"—favoring mothers in custody battles—can ignore a good father without due process or fair hearings. Still, my father fought and continued undeterred for years, trying to get custody of all eight of his children up until Brinly, the youngest, turned eighteen in 2013.

A week after the new family secret had been exposed, I was at my middle school chatting with Rachel and Christina. We heard my name called over the loudspeakers and I was summoned to the guidance counselor's office. I had never gotten in trouble at school before. Even though I struggled in my studies, I was a good student with passing grades.

Scared, I left my classroom and walked down the empty halls to the administration offices. I wondered what I had done wrong. Mr. Langston, the counselor, welcomed me into his office. He closed the door behind him. I flinched as he walked past me to sit in his desk chair.

"Christina, you can relax. You are not in trouble."

Oh, thank goodness, I thought, and I breathed a deep sigh of relief. Mr. Langston expressed his concern about the bruises on my arms and legs and the bald spots on my head that recently reappeared. I knew he wanted me to tell him who had done this to me, but I knew I would surely end up dead if I did. So I didn't say anything. I just let him talk. Then he said he had spoken to my father. I jumped up in excitement.

"You spoke to my father? Where is he? Is he okay? Is he coming to get me?"

"Christina, your father has been fighting for you while he has been in jail. He has been petitioning the courts for custody and trying to prove his innocence for the charge of hitting your mother. He knows you are being abused, and he has been calling from his jail cell to DCF asking for social workers to check on you. But every time the social workers fill out statements saying you are perfectly healthy and have no marks of abuse on you, your father's attempts to help you go unnoticed. I look at you every day and have seen the evidence with my own eyes. So when your father called me to ask for my help, I told him I would."

I tried to process all he was saying to me. I was overwhelmed, to say the least. Stumbling over my words, I asked when my father was coming to get me.

"Your father wants to come to get you, Christina. Your father needs your help and mine, and we need you to tell me what's going on at home so we can protect you."

The words had barely registered when the office door flew open. To this very day, I'm clueless as to how she knew I was there, but Mother stood in the doorway. She grabbed me by my collar, and yelled profanities at Mr. Langston, falsely accusing him of trying to molest me. Utter shock is how I'd describe his face . . . and mine. Mother and I abruptly walked out of the school and to the car. I was scared numb.

How did Mother know I was in his office? Why was my father in and out of jail so often for so many years?

My brain could not handle all the chaos that surrounded me. I got into the car and leaned my head against the window. I prayed to Jesus, asking him to take my life so I could be with him in heaven. I told him I would never do anything bad, and I would always love him if he would just come and take me home to be with him.

At home, Herman was at the kitchen table waiting for us. I didn't say a word. He jumped to his feet and began cursing at me for causing all the family disruptions. "You are nothing but trouble. You are such a little bitch. Mr. Langston can't save you. Do you really think we would let you get away? I know everything that happens in this town, you fool."

Mother grabbed me by my collar, snatching me up so fast that my knees buckled. She gripped my arms and dragged me to the closet in my bedroom. She threw me into the closet and turned off the light. I looked up at her silhouette before she slammed the door shut.

"You'll learn to keep your mouth shut," she said. "I know you're afraid of the dark, so I'm going to teach you not to be afraid. One day you'll thank me. After you think about what you've done to this family, I'll let you out. You are a filthy demon."

The first night in the dark closet, I wet myself, unable to get to the bathroom. I lost track of time. After what felt like days, my sister opened the door. The bright light hurt my eyes. I lifted my hand to cover them, and I saw her carrying something in her hands. She leaned over and shoved a bowl of Kraft macaroni and cheese toward me as if I were an animal. Dumbfounded and exhausted from being locked in a dark closet for so long, my anger raged. Without thinking, I kicked the bowl toward her.

"I am no one's dog, and I am your sister! Why aren't you helping me?"

I immediately regretted my choice. *What have I just done?*

My sister yelled for Mother. "She hit me; she hit me!"

Mother walked in. Catching sight of the pile of wire hangers on the floor, she grabbed one.

Arm raised high with her new weapon, she pulled me out of the closet. "How *dare* you touch your sister! She was kind enough to bring you food, and *this* is how you treat her? You selfish little girl! We'll teach you to mind your manners. You're so stupid that you'll never learn unless we beat you to death, will you?" When she was done, Mother dragged me back into the closet. She took away the bowl of food before shutting the door.

I was locked in the closet again without the ability to use the bathroom, shower, or eat. I became delusional. After the beating with the wire hanger, I think I temporarily lost a part of my mind. I couldn't understand why Mother hated me and why I was always doing bad things. I tried to be a good kid. I followed orders and minded my manners. How could Mother tell herself it was okay to treat me that way?

In that horrible moment, in all the deafening quiet, I felt around the closet floor and found a tube of "I Luv My Lips" lipstick that belonged to my older sister. I took off the plastic top, broke it in half, and began cutting my wrists. I wept hysterically for hours as I tried to kill myself with that dull piece of plastic. The fact that I couldn't even manage to take my own life upset me more than the beating I had received. I despaired. I was perpetually failing.

I can't read.

I can't be good enough for Mother.

I can't even kill myself.

Why am I so unwanted? No one will ever love me. Just let me die, God!

I passed out from exhaustion. When I came to, I had nothing more than a few cuts on my wrists and a pile of hair that I had pulled out of my head. Since God wouldn't allow me to die even when I had tried so hard to, maybe I was supposed to live. With that thought, I felt a calming presence come over me again, just like in the laundry room years ago. My mind and heart saw hope again. I experienced a supernatural hope for my life.

Despite all the traumas, I knew deep inside that life someday would be beautiful. I wasn't bad or crazy. I wasn't the reason my family was always in disarray. Hope overtook me. Lying in that dark closet, I set my mind to fight. To fight for my life. I would never give up and try to take my life again. The Lord spoke to my heart, giving me a glimpse of a happy future. I was left with hope—once again.

The night I got out of the closet, Mother and Herman told me I wouldn't be going to school anymore. Mother was going to homeschool me. Of course, she didn't, and I failed seventh grade. I wouldn't return to school until I was almost fifteen.

Over the years, Mother and Herman essentially imprisoned me. Confined to our house to keep others from asking about the bruises and the bald spots, I became the permanent babysitter, cook, and maid. I lost all contact with Rachel and Christina, which didn't surprise me because Mother made it impossible to have friends. One afternoon when I'd been hanging out with Rachel and Christina, Mother called the cops to tell them I was missing. Of course I was at Christina's house—and Mother knew that—but she scared their parents. As a result, the girls were forbidden to be around me.

So, after all of my strides, I found myself alone again, with no one to help me or rescue me. It was a devastating feeling. Mother and Herman tormented me for months after the middle school ordeal. I wasn't allowed to go to the bathroom without permission. I wasn't allowed to eat with the rest of the family. I was confined to my room and wasn't allowed to speak with my siblings. I felt trapped under the weight of Herman's shiny badge and Mother's hatred of her first marriage.

> Even if my father and mother abandon me,
> the LORD will hold me close.
> *Psalm 27:10 NLT*

CHAPTER 8

NJROTC

After Mother gave birth to her second child with Herman, she began farming out the rest of us to anyone who'd have us. It appeared to me that she only wanted to live with her new family of four, and that the eight kids she had with my father weren't worthy. Mother would lie to acquaintances and people she met at church, spinning stories of how she was a working single mother of eight. Of course these good-hearted souls took pity on her. So, in twos and threes, we would show up at strangers' homes with our black Hefty trash bags packed full. My siblings had been well acquainted with this type of couch surfing years before Mother would allow me to leave her grip. We'd leave for days or weeks, only to end up back on Mother's doorstep. Mother typically didn't provide any food or money for our care, which made for resentful Good Samaritans.

Shortly after I turned fourteen, Mother sent me, Carolina, and Jemma to live with the Violets, a young family in Ponte Vedra. The three of us were dropped off in the usual way—at the doorstep with our trash bags. Mrs. Violet opened the door and greeted us with a cheery tone.

"Come in, come in. Let me show you to your room." Her tight-lipped smile was forced, but as she grabbed Carolina's bag, I got a generally safe feeling from her. We filed in, one after the other, following her to our new room. Eyes open. Mouths shut. "Here we are. You can put your things in here. I'll show you around. Mr. Violet isn't home yet from work, and my children are still at school. You'll meet them later this evening."

We stood in front of the bunk beds like statues, staring at Mrs. Violet. She was a heavyset woman with a full figure, long dark hair, crimson lips, and square-frame glasses. She reminded me of my Italian aunts. She didn't have a loud voice, but everything else about her indicated that she was not to be ignored. Meeting her husband and children was terrifying for us because we didn't know what to expect.

Mrs. Violet had one boy who was a year younger than me, and two girls who were the same ages as my sisters. When Mr. Violet came home, his wife introduced us, and he shook our hands. He was tall and stocky, and he didn't say much. Being together in their living room felt awkward at first, but after a few weeks, we settled into a routine. We had food at every meal, enjoyed a well-kept house, and had two adults who seemed like they genuinely cared about us. Mrs. Violet was a God-fearing woman. She took us to church with her every week and gave each of us a Bible. I started reading mine right away even though I never understood anything it said.

After Mother pulled me out of school in seventh grade, I hadn't gone back and by the time we were with the Violets, it was nearly two years later. I only knew it was summer break because my sisters told me. But that summer, we were included in everything the Violets did. It was nice to be around a normal family.

One evening, Mrs. Violet came into our room and told me she was sending me to summer camp. *Summer camp?* I was shocked. *I get to go to camp?*

I sat straight up and closed my Bible. I stammered out a million questions. "Did you ask Mother if I could go? What is it for? When do I get to go? Can I really go? What will it be like?" She told me I would start high school after the summer break, and she wanted to help me get acclimated.

High school? Acclimated? That sounds painful. What does that even mean?

She then explained the meaning of *acclimated*. She assured me it was for my good. As she closed the door behind her, I lay back down in my bed and dreamed of what summer camp would be like.

Would I meet any nice girls like Rachel or Christina? Would I know what to do? What if they ask me to read something? What will I wear?

The next day, Mrs. Violet dropped me off at Allen D. Nease High School. A man wearing a crisp tan uniform covered in several awards walked over to us. Mrs. Violet signed me in and returned the clipboard to him. He held the clipboard in one hand, and his pen scribbled away as he balanced a coffee mug. He looked up, staring right at me. I was frozen. I silently pleaded for some direction.

"What are you still doing here? Get to the quarterdeck!" he scolded me impatiently.

I ran away as I yelled, "Yes, sir!" As I feverishly looked for the quarterdeck, I decided to ask anyone I could find to point me in the right direction. Running frantically around campus, rounding the corner of the locker room doors, I caught a glimpse through the breezeway of a giant concrete slab next to the gymnasium doors. A group of kids held themselves up in the push-up position. They moaned and groaned as if they were wounded animals, their sweat dripping onto the ground, men in uniforms hovering over them and yelling words in a foreign language.

Holy. Lord. Jesus. What is this?

As soon as I exited the breezeway, three men in uniforms made a beeline toward me. I had absolutely no idea what to do or what was going on.

All I knew was that I had found the quarterdeck.

And I also found that my summer camp was the Navy Junior Reserve Officers Training Corps (NJROTC) summer camp. While those first hours were terrifying, by the end of the day, it was the best time of my life. I was in love with all of it just from experiencing that pre-boot camp. I wanted to learn and be everything military.

I found out that the man with the clipboard whom I met upon arrival was named Master Chief Russ McFarland. He was a salty, gritty, no-nonsense sailor. Over time, he became like a father to me. His right-hand man was First Sergeant Daniel Calhoun. He was as intimidating as Master Chief, and I had immediate respect. I wanted to be just like him someday.

First Sergeant was a decorated Marine, and he taught our history classes, as well as what is known as "getting smoked." (This means endless pushups. Painful doesn't adequately describe how I felt during a hardy session with this war veteran!)

Mrs. Violet changed the course of my life when she signed me up for the Nease NJROTC summer boot camp in 2002. I never knew exactly why Mrs. Violet chose to send me there, but I suspect she thought I needed discipline and order. And who knows what terrible things Mother told her about me. But I'm forever grateful for the experience, and I know it saved me from all kinds of unimaginable horrors. I was a young girl with no proper guidance or protection, but I found both of those at NJROTC. I credit this program, as well as Master Chief, First Sergeant, and several other ROTC instructors for shaping me into the woman I am today.

Miraculously, I was able to make it to ninth grade even though I failed seventh and never went to eighth. After summer camp, I started my freshman year as a NJROTC Nease High School cadet. I was so proud to be a part of something so marvelous. I got involved in every activity I could. I was on the SEAL team, rifle team, drill ream, physical training (PT) team, sailing team, orienteering team, and color guard team—in addition to the cross-country and the track and field teams. My instructors took notice as I excelled in every area outside the classroom. Athleticism came naturally to me. It was something I never had the chance to tap into before.

I finally found something I was good at. Something that allowed *me* the opportunity to recognize *my* abilities.

Life with the NJROTC was a stark change from being under the thumb of Mother and Herman every waking moment. I still carried the wounds from the past few years, but they didn't seem to hurt as much. Instead of wishing and dreaming, I was busy working out with my teammates and studying the great Marine Corps lieutenant general Chesty Puller and Winston Churchill, my favorite military leader. My reading ability, although not on par with my peers, drastically improved during my first semester of high school. For not being in a classroom for years, I hardly skipped a beat.

Mrs. Violet's house was in Nease's district, so my bus came right to our street to pick me up. On the day when I had early morning practice, the new friends I made picked me up promptly at 5:30. After-school drill practice went until 6 p.m., and the late activities bus picked me up and dropped me off at my street again.

It was heaven.

I never once wondered how I would get to and from school practices. I was in complete bliss for the first semester of my high school career. I wore my uniform as many times a week as I could, polished my shoes every day, and learned every historical fact about the United States Navy and Marine Corps. I lived and breathed ROTC.

Master Chief often made time to tell me one-liners that, in the moment, seemed out of place. "It's okay to be wrong; it's not okay to be stupid." Or "Shut up and feed 'em hot dogs." Most of his one-liners didn't make any sense to me when he said them, but I'd reflect on them later. Although to this day I have no idea what the hot dog one is all about!

During cross-country practice, Master Chief and First Sergeant were our coaches. One day, Master Chief shouted, "Rugrat, get over here!"

Rounding the corner of the track, out of breath, I stopped just shy of running into him. I bent over, holding myself up with my hands on my knees. I lifted my gaze to his, sweat pouring off my forehead, gasping for air.

"Yes, Master Chief?"

"Lead, follow, or get out of the way," he said, his voice calm and certain. He lifted his coffee mug and took a sip, letting me know he had said all he wanted to say.

I replied, "Aye, aye, Master Chief." Without any idea of what he meant, I continued with my workout.

First Sergeant was exactly the same. He always gave me extra work or extra PT and never shied away from using me as the gold star example. Since it came from a man like him, I couldn't have been prouder to be recognized like that. He wore his uniform like he had just gotten off the battlefield. There was never a seam out of alignment. He was rugged, weathered, and terrifying . . . in a way that made me reach for my best.

I remember the day I wished First Sergeant was my dad. A bunch of cadets were out on the bulkhead, just in front of the classroom doors. True to my tomboy self, I was snorting snot from my nose to see how far I could get it to fly. I was surrounded by my peers, who were placing bets on my shining achievement. First Sergeant swiftly appeared—much to our dismay.

"Rugrat, what are you all doing out here on the bulkhead?" his voice echoed as we froze at attention. Unable to lie to this man, I summoned courage from deep within.

"We're having a spitting contest. And I'm in the lead, First Sergeant!" I sounded off as loudly as I could. Unsure of his reaction, my heart raced.

"At ease," First Sergeant said. The cadets looked at each other in confusion. "Let me show you how it's done."

He walked over, coughed up a huge loogie, and hawked it so far that it went into the tree line in front us. We all cheered like he'd just won the Super Bowl. We continued the contest, and at the end, it was me against him. The gaggle of us laughed and hollered as we all spat into the air. He won the contest—and also the award for coolest instructor.

It was the last day of school before the holiday break, and I was excited because we hadn't had a real Christmas in what seemed like years. I was never allowed to celebrate holidays or birthdays like my siblings, so I couldn't wait to get home that day to our new family. I got off the bus and began my half-mile walk down the street to the Violets' house. From a distance, I saw my two little sisters standing on the lawn. As I got closer, I could see the black trash bags sitting in the driveway.

I was crushed.

The Violets had packed up our things that day and waited for me to get home so they could drive us to Mother. I could only assume they were taking us back because the expense of three additional kids was too big of a burden. I believe that Mother had never sent money for groceries or living expenses (or if she did, it was far too little), and I'm sure Mr. and Mrs. Violet had to prioritize caring for their own children.

We hadn't seen Mother in months, but I was devastated to leave. I knew my life was over. Mother would never allow me to participate in ROTC. My two little sisters were crying as I walked up. I didn't cry—I just grabbed their hands. As we piled into the black Suburban, I prayed, "Lord, please help my baby sisters, and please let Mother let me go to Nease. Please help us, Lord." As we drove away from the only home that hadn't abused us, I felt hollowness begin to consume me once again.

> As for God, his way is perfect:
> the LORD's word is flawless;
> he shields all who take refuge in him.
> *Psalm 18:30*

CHAPTER 9

Sacrificial Prayers

The first few weeks with Mother were absolute misery. She had moved me, Christian, Abbeygail, and the youngest, Brinly, into a two-bedroom Vilano Beach condo. The rest of my siblings were living with other families and it was hard to keep track of who was where.

It was a long haul from the condo to Nease High School, or so Mother made me believe, so when I first moved back, I missed days of school. Every morning, we'd battle about me going to school. She refused to take me. Clutching my backpack with one strap over my shoulder, I begged her to drive me to school.

"If school is so important to you, find your own way," she insisted. "I need to get to work. You're too stupid for school anyhow. You'll never amount to anything. Give up already." Her eyes were cold as she walked past me and out the front door.

One evening, Master Chief called her on my behalf. I was so thankful. She agreed that if I could find my own rides to and from school, I could keep going. My education, or my well-being, for that matter, was never a priority for Mother. She put me in charge of all the household duties and caring for my youngest sibling as soon as Mrs. Violet dropped us off. Whatever Master Chief said to her that changed her mind about taking me out of school again must have been a miracle.

Praise the Lord! Truly!

Was it a constant battle to get her permission to compete in cross-country meets and ROTC drill meets? Yes, it was a nightmare, but somehow between the phone calls from Master Chief and First Sergeant, I was able to keep going to school. And thankfully my friends were still willing to drive the long haul to take me in the morning and then bring me back home.

Right away, I noticed that Mother had changed since I had last been with her. She was weepy. Chaotic. Unhinged on a whim. I'd never seen her this way. Cruel was her norm, but this time, she was full of despair because Herman broke up with her again. This time, he took both their children to his parents' house and refused to let her have any visitation. She was almost broken. She lost the man she traded her family for, and I'm sure her heart was hurting. At least, that's how I saw it. I found myself feeling very sorry for her.

She was alone.

This invited a new kind of chaos, and it was a nightly event. She would summon Christian and me out of our bunk beds and ask us to sleep in her bed with her. In a state of delusion, she told us how our father was in the bushes, coming to kill us in the night. Every creak, every faint noise, every movement, was an attack to kill us. She would only let us speak in her bathroom, because she said the house was bugged and that any information gleaned would be relayed back to our father. On some of her worst nights, she gave my little brother her revolver and me her Ka-Bar knife. She made us keep watch for intruders throughout the night while she slept. As a result, we'd both go to school dog-tired. If she heard too many noises after 9 p.m., she'd run all of us outside to her old BMW so we could get away from whomever she feared had been sent to kill us. She drove us all over St. Augustine, only parking for a few moments at a time until the sun came up. She was convinced at any moment we'd all be murdered.

The sleep deprivation started to wreak havoc on my body. I'd be sitting in class, mid-lecture, passed out on my desk. Learning at school had become such a joy for me, but now, chains bound me once again. I was unable to learn at school. Running at practice or doing drills after school became torture. I was exhausted.

Never once did I believe my father was out to hurt us. But after a few months of this routine, I did become fearful that *someone* was going to break in. I had nightmares that never allowed for a restful night. Mother had unraveled to the point that her abuses were a mix of physical beatings and this new psychological torment I'd never experienced before.

My second semester of my freshman year was dramatically different from the first. All of my teachers saw it, and they asked me pressing questions, just like Mr. Langston had done in middle school. Since my punishment for talking then was being yanked out of school for two years, I wasn't going to make that mistake twice. As the questions poured in, I became reclusive. First Sergeant noticed my new demeanor right away and called me Miss Stone-Cold. No laughing, no weeping, no emotion. I just did what I had to do to make it through each day of school. It was like standing at attention for hours. Except I wasn't called to attention. I was just browbeaten from the chaos that had been allowed back into my life.

My friend Matt drove me home many nights after school. If it hadn't been for him, I would've never completed my sophomore year. One evening, I got home really late, about eight o'clock, and noticed that Abbeygail and Christian had gone somewhere—I assumed to Grandmother's house for dinner. It wasn't unusual for them to go without me—I wasn't allowed over there after they found out about Talmon. I walked into the bedroom and saw Brinly lying on our bunk bed, drawing in a few books. Grandmother was no fan of toddlers, so only the older kids were welcome at her house now. I saw Mother's BMW out front, so I assumed she would be home, but there was no sign of her. The house was abnormally quiet.

I tended to Brinly for a few moments before I made my way upstairs to Mother's loft. Her room was a mess, but that was nothing out of the ordinary. Her purse was on the floor, confirming she was home. As I looked into the bathroom doorway, I saw Mother. She was in her pink lace nightgown, slumped on the floor against the cabinet sink. Her eyes were bloodshot red, and streaks of mascara ran down her face. She had a clove cigarette in one hand that was so long, it was a stick of ash. The bottle of liquid Vicodin in her other hand was almost empty, and there was a glass of red wine at her side. Some of the red wine from the bottle had spilled onto the tile. Ashes from her smoked cloves had formed piles on the floor.

"Mother, what's wrong? What are you doing?" I was at her side, attempting to comfort her.

"My. F—king. Life. Is. Over. I want to kill myself. I f—king hate you. This is all your fault. Herman took our babies and left me." She slurred every word with bitterness. Then she wept. She was desperate for another swig of the Vicodin, but I blocked her hand from her mouth. While she was pushing against me, she knocked over her glass of wine. The white lace trim that edged her silk nightgown turned red. She took her fiery clove and put it out on my skin, the singe digging deep into my arm.

"Mother, you just burned me!" I started crying. It was extremely painful. She looked up and laughed. It was the evilest thing I'd ever heard. But even as she was sitting there in all her ugliness, in all her mess, I loved her. And she still looked so beautiful to me.

"That's what you get for being a whore," she giggled. I put my arm under the faucet and turned on the cold water, trying to ease the burn.

"Mother, it's going to be okay. He will come back. He

always does. You can't kill yourself. What would the babies do?" I pleaded with her. I grabbed a washcloth to wipe her face. I sat down on the floor in front of her and wiped her tear-stained cheeks.

How do I convince her not to kill herself?

She screamed out of nowhere that her .45 was ready, and she was going to shoot herself in the mouth tonight when we were all sleeping. I became dreadfully afraid. I grabbed the Vicodin out of her hand and grabbed the wine bottle from the floor.

"What do you think you're doing, you little bitch?" she snarled as I rushed out of her bathroom. I ran downstairs to the kitchen sink. As I poured the medicine and wine down the drain, I exhaled with relief.

Thank you, Lord! Mother is still alive.

When I came back upstairs, I found Mother nearly lifeless, completely laid out on the bathroom floor. I knew she was barely conscious to begin with because her words were slurred, but I didn't think she was that bad off. I shook her and tried to wake her up. Nothing. Not even a cuss or a threat.

She just lay there, *lifeless.*

Terrified, I called 911 and grabbed the .45 from under her mattress, hiding it before the ambulance came. I cleaned up all the mess before they came to ensure that she didn't get taken away. When they arrived, I told them she accidently took medicine that made her this way. I didn't dare tell them she tried to kill herself.

After the overdose, Mother promised she'd pick me up on days she didn't work late. This was either to keep me quiet or because she felt some guilt for the way she treated me. Rides were hard to come by, so this was especially exciting for me. As I sat on the sidewalk after drill practice, like many days before, I was the last student on campus. Nearly all of the teachers had left for the day, and the school grounds and parking lots felt like a ghost town.

Waiting for Mother after school always filled me with shame. For hours, I watched parents load up their kids with love, eager to get home. Pickup after pickup. Knowing that Mother hated me hurt my heart.

Why can't she love me like all the other parents love their kids?

Most nights she said she would come get me, she forgot. This left my teachers to find a remedy, like giving me a ride or paying for a taxi to take me home. The only other student who stayed until dusk was Tim Tebow, the most popular boy in school. Waiting for Mother, I'd sit on the sidewalk and watch him practice football with his dad and the football coaches on the field across the parking lot. They gave him extra one-on-one coaching. Every girl in school talked about him, and every boy was his friend.

Every time I see this boy, his father is with him.

I knew this boy's father loved him very much, as if he were a treasure to be protected. He was always standing close to coaches as they directed him. Watching from the distance, I dreamed I was like him.

That I was special—like him—and that Mother loved me.

As I drifted off into daydreaming, I was abruptly interrupted.

"Young lady, what are you doing out here? Everyone has gone home."

Startled, I looked up. Tim's father had walked all the way across the football field through the parking lot and up the sidewalk to ask me this very firm question. I was intimidated, to say the least. I sputtered out, "Yes, sir. Mother sometimes forgets me, but I know she'll be here soon. I just wait here until she comes." His face went from a stern, concerned expression to one of complete sorrow.

He looked me in the eyes and asked, "Can I pray for you?" I nodded my head in acceptance and hastily lowered my head. As he prayed, my heart saw a glimpse of hope. It was something I had lost, but now found once more. There are some things we all need to be reminded of, and hope is one of them. It can be misplaced for days or months or even years. Hope is a daily necessity for a thriving life.

Mr. Tebow's son was there after school because he was special; I was there after school because I was an afterthought. I felt so much shame every time Mr. Tebow prayed for me, and I wished I could be like Tim. Maybe Mr. Tebow saw something in me that no one else did—not even myself—and that's why he took the time to pray for me.

Mr. Tebow may have forgotten about that broken little girl sitting on the sidewalk late in the evening, but I will never forget his willingness to offer prayers for me. It still blesses my heart to this day. It reminds me to heed the call to pray for others.

In the middle of my sophomore year, Mother and Herman got back together again. He wanted to take Mother on a trip to celebrate, a luxurious adventure to Turkey. She began doling the kids out immediately. I was sixteen by this time, still living and breathing ROTC, dreaming of the days when I would serve in the greatest fighting force known to mankind. Master Chief told me that if I told Mother I disliked taking orders from him, she would let me stay with him while she was away.

Genius.

So I learned the art of reverse psychology. As instructed, I started making comments about how Master Chief was hard on me, always giving me more work than other cadets. When Master Chief made a call to her a few days later, he had miraculously convinced Mother to let me stay with him while she was away.

Joy!

This was going to be so awesome. I was staying with Master Chief and Mrs. McFarland for two weeks! Endless double chocolate chip cookies were all I could think about. At school, she always made them for the cadets—and she always gave me a secret stash to take home. She was one of the best ROTC moms. At every drill meet, every practice, every event, this woman made our lives so much better. She tended to each of us like we were her own. I loved her.

Master Chief had pulled it off. Finally, I'll get to be with two people who cared about me, dare I say loved me, for a few days. Plus, I wouldn't have to worry about school rides or whether I could compete in the upcoming drill meets, because Master Chief was running the show!

Just glorious relief.

Right before I was going to stay with Master Chief, he went to the hospital for a bump on his head. It turned out to be stage 4 skin cancer.

I was shattered at this discovery. We all were. First Sergeant and his wife, Mrs. Calhoun, agreed without hesitation to take me into their home. First Sergeant was a father figure to me too, and Master Chief was his best friend. They lived just a few houses from each other, so this was a painful time for all of us. A few months later, I'd hold Master Chief's hand one last time as he lay in his bed, dying. Up until this point, I had never lost anyone to death. I cried for days. Weeks on end. It was a pain I had never experienced before.

Different. Deep. Permanent.

With my vast knowledge of different types of pain, I thought I was equipped to deal with any amount or form. But some pain cannot be prepared for. In an instant, it crushes one's heart—a heart that can only be made well again through much weeping and time.

When I was staying with First Sergeant and Mrs. Calhoun, Mother made no attempt to contact me. Instead of leaving me at their house for two weeks, as agreed, I was there for two and a half months. Every attempt by First Sergeant to contact Mother failed. But I'd grown comfortable being where I was. After the second week of having my own bed, three meals a day, and two parents who loved me, I broke the cardinal rule:

keeping our family secrets secret. I told First Sergeant and Mrs. Calhoun everything. Every last detail.

They told me they would never let anyone hurt me again and that they loved me. They promised to keep me away from Mother. First Sergeant confessed he already knew I was being abused. He said he and Master Chief had been working on a plan to get me out alive.

That Thanksgiving, I was in the kitchen helping Mrs. Calhoun clean up and wrap all the food we had prepared. It was glorious to be in the kitchen doing normal things and listening to holiday music! I loved her very much. She was a great mom to her kids.

Knock. Knock. Knock.

Why was someone knocking so ferociously on the front door? I could hear it all the way from the kitchen. First Sergeant quickly answered the door. To his surprise and mine, a Jacksonville police officer greeted him.

Here we go.

I knew this was about me. I grew up with the thin blue line always knocking on our doors. Walking to the front living room, I could hear the officer tell First Sergeant and Mrs. Calhoun that Gale Smith—Mother—had reported her daughter Christina as a runaway and that she had run away to this address. He was here to take her back to her mother.

First Sergeant and his wife had looks of complete disbelief. I wasn't taken aback in the least.

First Sergeant replied with firmness. "What are you talking about? Her mother left her here over two months ago, saying she was going on a work trip for two weeks, and we haven't heard so much as one word from her. I think you should sit down, sir, and listen to what is going on here."

The police officer and First Sergeant sat down and talked for more than two hours. By the end of it, we were all filling out affidavits. Meanwhile, another group of officers showed up. This time, Mother was with them. She came with one of Herman's friends from the St. Augustine Police Department. She demanded that I come home and insisted that I had run away.

The Jacksonville police officer told me if I was brave enough to write down what I had told the Calhouns about my family in the affidavit, I would never be hurt by Mother again. I could stay with First Sergeant, and he would make Mother leave the premises. Afraid I was going to get killed for what I was about to do, I took the officer's pen, held First Sergeant's hand, and wrote down as best I could what Mother had done to me during the past sixteen years.

Thanksgiving that year was a disaster.

But it was also the year I was finally free from Mother and Herman.

"Be strong and courageous.
Do not fear or be in dread of them,
for it is the LORD your God who goes with you.
He will not leave you or forsake you."
Deuteronomy 31:6 ESV

CHAPTER 10

The Adjustment

After my affidavit, the State of Florida finally took six of us—me, my three younger sisters, and my two younger brothers—away from Mother. It took seven years from the first abuse investigation to finally be free from harm. We were placed as wards of the State of Florida, and I was ecstatic. (My two brothers from Herman and Mother's marriage remained in her care.)

Sadly, it didn't last long. Less than a year later, after she completed a few mandatory parenting classes, the St. Augustine court awarded her full custody of the six of us again.

With one caveat.

She stated in one of the court documents that although she was thankful to have her children back, she regretted to inform the court she would be refusing parental rights over me. She didn't want me. The judge allowed her to sever parental rights over me, releasing me to the State of Florida until I was eighteen.

With a single signature, the City of St. Augustine allowed

Mother to choose her children. For me, this was just fine, but for everyone else, it was a gross injustice. My siblings returned to the dysfunction that I believe still haunts them. And I have never seen Mother again.

Since I had been staying with the Calhouns already, the State gave them temporary custody as a non-relative placement. I was in heaven. First Sergeant and Mrs. Calhoun gave me my own room, food whenever I wanted, new clothes, new shoes, and a new backpack. They even got me my own night-light after I had woken them up with my nightmares. They gave me everything I had ever wanted. Rides to and from school and practice were now a breeze, and I never waited for hours after school. I never had to worry if I was going to be allowed to compete in any school events. They would gladly take me, pay for my athletic equipment, and watch me as I tried my best at being an all-star athlete. In just a few months, I fell in love with them.

Having a new child in the home must have been difficult for the three Calhoun children. The Calhouns treated me to new shoes and clothing because my things were old and tattered. I worried that the children felt jealous and resented the intrusion into their family. A girl coming from nothing into a home with three other children who had always had everything was going to be difficult. Probably more difficult than anyone thought. I was so used to sharing everything with my siblings—not that we ever had much—that I never thought twice about using my new roommates' stuff. I didn't realize that people actually got to have their own things. We ended up having weekly family meetings about how to get along with each other.

Mrs. Calhoun took care of me with great tenderness. Soon after I moved in, she went into my closet for something, and to her surprise, she found a hoard of food I'd hidden for safe-keeping. I'd grown up with locks on the fridge when there was actually food in it, and most of the time, we had to find our own way to eat. I never knew what it was like to have access to a fully stocked fridge. I swear First Sergeant and Master Chief first stole my heart by bringing an extra lunch with them to school. And they did it every single day.

So even though I was allowed to eat whenever I wanted, it didn't translate into *safe*. I had yet to learn what that word meant. (I'm still learning what that word means.) It never once occurred to me that the food in their fridge or pantry would be there the next day. And this pantry! It was huge. I'd never seen a pantry so filled with food. I snuck in there, literally as a thief in the night, grabbing what I could that would keep in my closet. Finding my stash was an awakening for Mrs. Calhoun. It was a glimpse at what trauma does to a person.

That day, I bounced into the kitchen to see what she had set out for us. After-school snacks were a real thing after all! As I stuffed my face with carrots and ranch dressing, she asked to speak to me upstairs privately in her bedroom.

Dread overcame me.

With tears in her eyes, she pulled out the boxes of Fig Newtons (my favorite) and Wheat Thins (another of my favorites).

I lowered my head in shame.

Her voice was calm with empathy. "Chris, I'm not sure why you're taking food out of the kitchen and hiding it in your room, but you don't need to do this anymore. Okay?" Her voice filled with sadness.

Was she weeping for me? She wasn't upset with me at all!

I'd never known such compassion. I didn't know what to say. Grabbing her, giving her a hearty embrace, I cried, thankful for her kindness. I promised not to steal food out of the kitchen anymore. In that moment, I saw her heart. It was kind. It was good. It was brave enough to allow me to be in her home, even with all my weaknesses.

A year later, during my junior year, the state's attorney came knocking on our door, summoning me to the St. Augustine courthouse. I had no idea what it was about, and neither did the Calhouns.

A few days later, we walked into the state's attorney's office and I felt a bitter breeze in the room. It was as if my body knew something bad was happening. The attorney asked us to sit down. She explained that Talmon had written a lengthy letter in which he confessed that he abused me.

What?

To this day, I have no idea why he'd confess.

Overwhelmed with questions, fear, and shame, I didn't know how to react. My eyes welled up with uncontrollable anger, and as tears ran down my face, I shouted question after question: "What? Is he in jail? What is happening?"

The attorney said that for her to verify the legitimacy of

the letter, she had to read a few parts to me. She got through one sentence before I burst into hysterical tears.

"Such disgust! How can you read this letter aloud to me? In front of Mr. Calhoun!" I continued to shout. "Why are you doing this to me?"

I was so ashamed and embarrassed and beside myself.

Is she looking at me like I had something to do with him raping me?

Why did she read the part about him saying I had said yes to all the things he did to me?

I looked at the attorney in disbelief. "I was nine years old! What is wrong with everyone? Do they really believe him?"

It was like being raped again—except people were watching.

I was a mess. She stopped after a few more sentences. She declared that she didn't need to go any further; she had all she needed. Looking me in the eyes, she asked me what his punishment should be. Confused as to why she would ask me or why I would have the authority to give him punishment, I told her this—in these very words: "He should suffer the way I have suffered. He should go to jail for ruining my childhood." I gasped for air between each word.

Mrs. Calhoun took me by the shoulder, leaned into me, and said, in a tone that took me aback, "You are being too emotional. Step out into the hall. We will handle this."

It was as if she was scolding me. I felt slighted and so confused.

I'll never forget how she sounded that day.

As Mrs. Calhoun escorted me out the door, I went numb. Unable to process what had just happened, I wept hysterically in the hallway. I feared that everyone believed it was my fault, just like Mother said.

Six years after my father's initial reports of my having been sexually abused, my uncle had walked into the St. Augustine Police Department with a "confession" letter and turned himself in. He wrote that I had said okay to all the horrible things he did to me. He said it had only happened a few times.

Classic pedophile confession.

After hearing Talmon's startling revelation, the St. Johns County Sheriff's Office began an investigation. I can only imagine what Herman, Mother, and my grandparents where thinking—or saying—and what all the officers, social workers, and other "expert" witnesses of Father's custody battle thought when they heard about this "confession."

I have no idea why he confessed, and I have no idea if anyone actually believed that I, as a child, gave him permission to do those horrible things.

The investigation quickly and quietly went away. And by quietly, I mean Talmon was told to hand over his confession letter and to write out an affidavit, which he did. The case started out as a capital sexual battery but was eventually pleaded down to a felony battery. He was given two years' probation, community service, and less than a year in county jail for brutalizing me from the time I was nine years old to almost thirteen years old. They charged him with felony battery, as if he had gotten into a bar fight.

In Florida, a sexual crime committed by a person older than eighteen against a minor younger than twelve is considered a capital felony, with a potential sentence of life in prison, placement on the sexual offenders' list, and a slew of other substantial punishments.

But that awful day at the state's attorney's office where they revictimized me, I felt they were declaring that the factual evidence of the crimes committed against me never amounted to a hill of beans.

This is what is most disturbing.

It is gross negligence like this that makes my blood boil for justice—if not for me, then for every other little girl or boy who has been ravaged by the cankers of this world without being allowed justice. Sexual perversion is a global pandemic. It spreads like the stench of death from a rotten corpse with every violent attack and every pornographic image.

This reality—this unbelievable injustice that I endured—is a big part of the reason why I'm telling my story to the world.

The next day, Mrs. Calhoun said I wouldn't be going to school. I had to go to the doctor. I had gone to the dentist just a month before, so I assumed it would be something like another routine checkup. I got dressed, got in the car, and went with her to the doctor. We arrived at a big building. I couldn't see any signs, so I didn't know what type of doctor it was.

A receptionist took my ID information and wrote my name on the sign-in sheet. We then sat down in front of a coffee table filled with magazines.

"Mrs. Calhoun, what kind of doctor am I seeing?" I asked with jittery anxiety.

She said, "We're at the OB-GYN."

I had never heard of that before, so I shrugged my shoulders and asked her what that meant. "It's a gynecologist, a doctor for females to check their female parts. Everything will be fine. They just need to make sure you're healthy." What I didn't fully understand until later is that I had been ordered by the State of Florida to be examined in connection with the abuse by Uncle Talmon.

I was horrified.

I had never been to a gynecologist before. I didn't even know what it was until she told me. I couldn't believe what she was saying.

"Wait, I don't understand. That means someone has to look at me down there?"

Her look told me yes.

"Mrs. Calhoun, please don't do this. Please don't let them look at me." I began crying. "Please don't let them look at me naked."

I couldn't understand why I was here. I had never had sex with a boy or even been naked in front of a boy. *Don't you only go to this type of doctor if you have sex or if you get pregnant by a boy?*

When they called my name, I was weeping and scared out of my skin. Two nurses came over and directed me toward an exam room. Mrs. Calhoun followed as I begged them not to put me in that room.

"Mrs. Calhoun, please! Don't let them do this to me. I'll be good. I promise. I won't steal food anymore. Please don't do this to me!"

But Mrs. Calhoun remained quiet and calm. And unemotional.

By this time, the entire office was staring at me, peeping out of the doors and leaning over nurses' stations. I paid no mind to them. I pleaded for my life without hesitation. Three nurses held my arms and legs as they forced me into the room with a table that looked like a death trap. Torturous-looking metal handles stuck up from the bottom of the table, like iron snares for one's feet. A flimsy sheet of paper covered the table from top to bottom.

What in the world was this place?

My eyes scanned the room to see what clues I could pick up. A metal tray filled with needles, giant cotton swabs, and other evil-looking tools I had never seen before were lined up neatly with a box of gloves. When I saw that tray, I screamed so loud that the doctor came in and yelled at me.

"Young lady, you need to calm down right now!"

I stopped yelling, but I certainly didn't stop crying. Mrs. Calhoun helped me take my pants off. The nurses in the room told me to sit on the table, to take off my underwear, and to cover myself with a cotton robe. Closing the door, they stepped out of the room. I began begging Mrs. Calhoun again not to make me do this. She said the state was making me do this and that I didn't have a choice. It would be over soon. I would be okay. She helped me—while I was still crying profusely—take off my underwear and covered me in the gown they gave us. I sat on the chair that felt more like a coffin and locked my hands over my legs, holding the gown down so no one could see me.

The two nurses walked back in and asked me to lie down.

I couldn't. I couldn't do it.

Mrs. Calhoun and the other nurse had to physically hold me down as the other nurse pushed my bottom toward the end of the chair.

"Mrs. Calhoun, don't you love me? Don't let them do this! Please, please, Mrs. Calhoun, don't make them do this to me," I said in a deep whimper of misery. Begging for them not to make me spread my legs, I shouted, "Noooo! You're hurting me. Stop. Please stop!"

Mrs. Calhoun didn't say a word.

A nurse moved to the end of the chair to put my feet in the metal holsters. Mrs. Calhoun gripped my hand and held my upper body down as they called in another nurse. The four women held me down as they took a pap smear.

By the end of it all, I was groaning in deep agony while crying. By this time, Mrs. Calhoun was crying too. The nurses were doing all they could to hold back their tears. None of them wanted to make me do what they had just made me do. Apparently, the State of Florida demanded that I have an STD test done, effectually re-raping me due to the state's attorney's desire to verify the legitimacy of the "confession" letter and to comply with standard protocol.

It was one of the most traumatic experiences I've ever had.

After this painful experience, I trusted no one. I became colder than ice. I got a new nickname at school: Ice Queen. Sometimes I replay these moments in my mind. I try to understand how people could have said and done what they did. I never found a common thread, even as a grown woman. The memories feel like betrayal. *How could someone do that to another human being? I was sixteen. Still just a kid. A young girl. They should have better prepared me. They should have done things differently.*

Things were not the same for me at the Calhouns' house after that. I grew further away from the family. I became their invisible fourth child, always slipping into my room as soon as I got home from school. I stopped participating in family events. I knew that when I turned eighteen, I could legally do anything I wanted. So I began to plan my great escape.

I turned eighteen the first semester of my senior year. The start of school came with numerous changes, much like every year before that. I moved out of the Calhouns' house with the same things I came with, including my black trash bags. I moved in with one of my NJROTC friends, which kicked off my year of couch surfing. The Calhouns were very upset with me and probably unsure of why I was leaving. They even called a school meeting with the principal to convince me to come back, but I couldn't. I loved them, but I wasn't emotionally capable of understanding that they loved me, so I ran away.

Far away.

Isn't that what you do when you believe someone doesn't love you the way you love them?

Running is easy—especially when you feel you've been wounded. It didn't help that my communication skills were atrocious. I didn't have the skill set that lets a person dig deep into their feelings and share them. Cultivating that ability took me some years. I only knew how to shut off and move on. It was easier for me to be silent than to express emotion. Hence, the nicknames Miss Stone-Cold and Ice Queen.

After I ran away, I didn't have an exact plan other than wanting to serve my country as an officer in the military. I began couch surfing while I worked on getting my driver's license. I would drive friends' cars to and from school, and I volunteered to be the designated driver at parties to practice my skills. No one knew I didn't know how; they just handed over the keys. In addition to school, cross-country practice, track and field practice, and NJROTC, I worked two jobs—one at Smoothie King and one at Village Inn, a restaurant similar to IHOP. When I could, I got rides with one of the four people who became my best friends: Matt, Kendall, Buster—all of whom I met at school—or Jay, a guy I worked with at Smoothie King.

Working at Smoothie King after school and Village Inn as a waitress on weekends was enlightening. I quickly learned the meaning of a hard-earned dollar. Although I worked part-time at Firehouse Subs when I lived with the Calhouns, I never needed the money then. It was different being an adult and needing money to survive. My mind was flooded with memories of times when my sisters and I found odd jobs around the neighborhood just so we could buy groceries.

Although it was difficult on us, one of my proudest moments as a child actually arose from neglect and abandonment. Mother had been gone for almost a week, and we had no food in the house. RaeLynne was at a friend's house, so Abbeygail and I began plotting a dinner we'd never forget. We'd saved $17.86 from babysitting neighborhood kids. We took a busted rolling suitcase with a broken zipper and walked across highway US 1 to the Winn-Dixie store.

Abbeygail was in charge of managing the money, and I looked for food that didn't require cooking, since our electricity had been shut off. We ended up buying two Kraft Mac & Cheese boxes, three cans of tuna, a gallon of milk, a jar of peanut butter, and a loaf of bread. We were short on money, so the women working the counter covered us for thirty-five cents. We couldn't stop smiling as we walked across the highway with our suitcase filled with food. It was like Christmas morning.

Did a car *almost* hit us? Sure! But *did* a car hit us? No, praise the Lord!

We walked home, knocked on the neighbor's door, cooked the mac and cheese, and brought it back to our house. We added in the tuna and filled each of our plastic cups to the brim with milk. We rejoiced in silence with cheerful grins of success. It was heaven. We fed our younger brothers and sisters until they were full, and then we ate the rest. We tucked in little Brinly, Noah, Jemma, Carolina, and Christian. That night felt so good. I knew they were fed. Abbeygail and I often gave up our food for them, but that night we *all* got to eat.

After an almost two-year reprieve with the Calhouns, I'd forgotten the painful times of scrounging for money to buy groceries, but it all came back to me during my senior year. When I couldn't find a ride, I'd take taxis to and from school. I wanted to graduate more than anything. I was so close! I wasn't going to let anything keep me from walking across the platform to accept my diploma. I worked tirelessly to make sure I was at school and after-school practices.

I'm not sure how I managed it, but I was captain of the cross-country and track and field teams during this time. I also held the prized position of NJROTC community service officer for our battalion. I handled toy drives, community fund-raisers, and school fund-raisers for our national competitions. I had more work than a bee in a hive during my senior year! Somehow, between all the couch surfing and taxi rides, I managed to take the walk with my peers. I didn't get to go to prom, but I did graduate from high school—which is basically the same thing for a girl in my situation.

During my chaotic high school career, I achieved more than ten varsity letters; twelve national first-place awards; several first-place prizes in state competitions, including a rifle competition, which was my most prized accomplishment; a few congressional awards; and countless other awards for my achievements. All I ever wanted was to serve as an officer in the military, like most of my NJROTC peers wanted to do. More than half of my class joined the military and became part of the most elite fighting force in the world. Out of that half, several went to college for ROTC or to one of the prestigious military academies.

We had all worked so hard during our four years of NJROTC for this purpose. With that in mind, I applied for the ROTC college scholarship, hoping to make my dream of becoming an officer in the military come true. Going through the process was extremely disheartening. Most of my peers, with their 4.0s and brilliant academic careers, were also applying for the three coveted spots. I knew my grades would not get me in, but I was certainly going to give it my best shot. Maybe something would happen and I'd be selected. Master Chief always told me, "You don't know 'til you try." He also said, "If you ain't cheating, you ain't trying"—so there's that!

A few days later, I was politely informed I didn't make the cut. For a few days after that, my spirit was broken. I wanted to be an officer so badly. NJROTC was the only thing I was truly good at. I had worked for four years with that goal in view. Knowing I couldn't afford college on my own, I wept alone in the NJROTC conference room. After I cried, I started planning my next move toward greatness. I wasn't going to give up. I would press in and press on.

With all the opportunities to fall in with the wrong crowd in high school or to do something incredibly stupid, trouble couldn't find me. First Sergeant Calhoun, Master Chief McFarland, and instructors like Captain Williams, Captain Young, Master Chief Duffy, and Gunny Hanson already had.

Praise the Lord for that frightening day at pre-boot camp my freshman year! My life might have turned out very differently if I hadn't had these men leading me on at every turn.

A week after I graduated, I took the driver's test at the Department of Motor Vehicles for the third time and passed. Finally, all those times of being the designated driver paid off! With my diploma, brand-new Florida driver's license, and a small wad of cash I had saved up over the summer, I purchased my first car—a two-door Chevy Cavalier, painted a bright yellow.

I named her "Sunny" since she so clearly deserved the name.

I was so excited. My very first car! I drove around for hours that day. When I returned to the room I was renting in a double-wide on the outskirts of town, my good mood was once again tested. The owners told me they found someone who would pay a higher rent, and therefore they had no choice but to let that person have the room. I had to leave. They were sorry, and so was I. I packed up the few things I had, cramming Sunny to the brim. I drove to the pier, where I parked to sleep for the night.

Sadness began to fill my heart, and I wept.

Mother's words filled my mind. Shame covered me as I tried to sleep in the front seat of my car.

Maybe she was right. Maybe I won't *amount to anything.*

Will I ever become a military officer?

Am I only good at cleaning?
Who is going to love me now—now that I have nothing to offer?
Lord, what am I going to do now?

> Trust in the Lord with all your heart
> and lean not on your own understanding;
> in all your ways submit to him,
> and he will make your paths straight.
> *Proverbs 3:5–6*

CHAPTER 11

Sunny

It was the end of December when I moved into Sunny. The chill in the air had already come; winter was here. Driving around the first few nights to find safe places to park was a stressful task. I was so afraid of someone breaking in while I was sleeping. I still worked at the Village Inn, but I was looking for another job that paid better. I knew if potential employers found out I was living in my car, they wouldn't hire me, so I conveniently forgot to mention that part. I applied at the Casa Monica Hotel in downtown St. Augustine as a valet attendant. To my surprise, they hired me a day later.

I was over the moon! I bet people made so much money at that place. It was all so fancy—even the bathrooms. It took me only a few days to figure out how to get dressed, washed up, and prepared for a work shift in two feet of space. The key is organization. You've got to be completely organized in a small space to maximize efficiency. Everything has a home. Everything belongs in its home when not in use. Toiletries in this bag, clean clothes in another, dirty clothes in the trunk, and baby wipes on deck 24/7. Organization!

Before my valet shift, I'd sneak into the hotel's bathrooms and wash up with their fancy hand towels, making sure no one saw me. Showers, however, were more complicated. I didn't really think about where I was going to shower every day until one day, I realized that showers are only available to those with a home—or enough money for a hotel room. Then, during my second week of work at Casa Monica, a lightbulb went off. There were showers at the beach!

My plan was to get up at sunrise to paddle out on my surfboard at Vilano Beach. I had grown up surfing on Vilano, so I knew its quick sets and crushing shore breaks. There was nothing more beautiful than a Vilano sunrise. The glorious sun peeked its rays over the horizon while my hands and feet dangled in the ocean water. The water is always picture-perfect in the early morning. Like plate glass.

So that morning, I paddled out and forgot all my woes. Beach showers had recently been installed at the access point for all the beachgoers. The only other people out that early were surfers or older women on morning walks. I saw the new beautiful outdoor showers as I came to shore, and I took the opportunity for a shower in my salty bathing suit.

Hallelujah!

A clean shower! And thus I began my daily wash at the beach access. I was washing clothes and drying them at friends' houses when I could and doing my best to keep clean for my work shifts. Casa Monica was so luxurious that

I couldn't believe I was working for them. It was even more unbelievable that I was a valet attendant who had just recently gotten her license. Driving fancy cars for fancy people was a delight. While parking cars, I'd dream that the vehicle was mine and I was headed for easy living and elaborate board meetings in extravagant hotels.

When I wasn't at my valet job, I was working late-night shifts at the Village Inn that lasted from six in the evening until four in the morning—what we called "the drunk shift." All the people who'd boozed throughout the night came to us for our trademark pie and, of course, our exceptional service. I made great money from midnight to 4 a.m. Drunk people love pie. And they always loved my southern hospitality.

Getting off work so late in the night, or so early in the morning, was difficult for me. I walked to Sunny and drove far away to one of my secluded spots to change my clothes in the front seat. I washed my body with a baby wipe and tried to sleep. During the winter, it got pretty cold in the car. I bundled up with all the sweaters and socks I had. Music was a huge part of my life, so my CD player became my dearest possession. That and my Bible.

The Bible was a gift from my dearest friend, Jay, who became like my brother. He'd given it to me, with my name inscribed on it, during my senior year of high school. I read it every night. The Bible comforted me and helped me feel less scared.

In my senior year, I'd become very involved in reading the Word of God, and my relationship with Jesus Christ grew into a daily walk with him. When I became homeless, all I did was pray and shout out promised Scripture back to God.

I am your daughter, am I not? You said your children don't beg for bread, Lord!

This doesn't look like the goodness of the Lord in the land of the living to me, God!

You love me? This is love? All I've ever done is the right thing, and this *is my reward? I thought you had great plans for me. Is it to be alone in a world that nobody wanted me in to begin with? GOD? Are you there?*

I had words with the Maker of heaven and earth. I knew his Word. I knew him! How could this be, then? Me living out of a car? I barely had enough money to eat after paying my car payment and insurance. How could my Father in heaven allow me to suffer like this?

It would take more than a decade to answer that very honest question.

After surviving the winter and spring living out of Sunny, summer revealed the beauty of high humidity inside a car without AC. As weeks became months, I found it increasingly hard to maintain normalcy. Staying clean became more trying, washing clothes more difficult, sleeping more disturbed. Work shifts became exhausting. Trying to save money to get a place to live became a crushing weight I felt I would never manage. Summer was a harsh drought on my weary soul. Optimism turned into angry disappointment. Talking with the Lord was more of a begging whimper to help me get out of this mess. My soul was crushed. I didn't understand how this could have happened to me and why God was allowing it.

One afternoon, I was driving and saw Christian walking with a friend to the Jiffy Food Store. I hadn't seen him in years! I was immediately overcome with joy and sadness. I missed him and loved him so much, but I knew he was still under Mother's influence. I pulled over and called out his name. We hugged and talked for a few minutes. He commented that Sunny looked like a small yellow school bus. It was an emotional time for both of us.

A few nights later, when it was hotter than hot, I parked Sunny along the beach and walked over to a fancy beach cabana that the hotels set out for their guests. Christian happened to be walking by, noticed my car, and followed my footprints in the sand to find me lying in the cabana.

"Tina!" he said with joy. His eyes were sweet, and he smiled. His tone was that of tender kindness.

"Christian, what are you doing out here?" My face betrayed my embarrassment. My voice cracked with shame.

Without another word, he lay in the cabana next to me. His presence was enough. He blessed my heart to the fullest. No words needed to be spoken. Together, we looked up into the glorious galaxy of stars above. We watched the crashing waves lit up by the full moon, and we lay under the canopy of starlight and drifted off to sleep with the sound of the roaring ocean and the cool breeze.

Sunrise crept out from behind the waters and woke us up. The heat was already sweltering, so we went for a dip in the ocean. After we swam for a good bit, I asked Christian if he was hungry. Knowing neither of us had money and were hungry, I suggested we walk into the hotel like we were guests for the free breakfast. I mean, we looked like tourists in our bathing suits coming in from the cabana hut!

We both were nervous to walk in, but we were more hungry than scared. I went straight to the continental breakfast and served myself. Then I helped my little brother. He wanted to rush out, but I told him, "No! Then they'll know we aren't real guests. We have to sit at the table, and no one will say anything to us, I promise."

No one said one word to us. I thought for sure after second and then third helpings they would, but not one peep!

Summer was a different kind of fight for me—not only physically, but mentally and spiritually. Several nights, in the wearisome summer heat, I was awakened by dreams—dreams of great things. Great things that I was doing, such as standing on stage in front of thousands dressed like a first lady. I was speaking to encourage their hearts. I had dreams of writing a book—a book that would help millions reach for joyous hope in dark nights of grief. I dreamed of traveling the globe as an ambassador for human rights, creating laws and nonprofits to help others flourish after experiencing tremendous suffering.

I had dreams of what seemed to be my life ten, twenty, thirty years down the road. They were intense, vivid, colorful, detailed dreams of a glorious life. After waking up from these beautiful dreams, I was enraged. It felt like God was giving me these dreams, which was confusing and downright annoying.

Are you kidding me, Lord? These dreams are ridiculous. They're so far from where I am! You realize I'm living in my car, right? There is no way that kind of life could be mine. Stop giving me these dreams!

Night after night, I had dreams of a new life. In my dreams, I lived sweetly under the sun. I enjoyed a meal at the table with my entire family. I smiled at the world with great expectation. And morning after morning, I woke up, wept, and begged the God of the universe to take these nonsensical dreams away from me.

Eventually, I gave up asking God to take them away and decided to just accept them. Soon after, they took hold of my heart. God's dreams gave me permission to start dreaming on my own. That's when I started to love all the dreams I had. I loved the dreams of my future husband. Of my children. And of the nonprofit I would start for abused girls and boys. I became a dreamer. It was a lovely escape from the reality I was currently living. I wrote down all my dreams and anchored them to correlating Scripture. They were like little treasure chests filled with promises that would one day be mine. Working two jobs, reading my Bible, and dreaming my dreams became my life as I lived out of Sunny.

One day while I was working at Village Inn, Danny Swanson's parents came in with his brothers. Danny wasn't with them, but seeing his family warmed my heart. I was flooded with memories of all those lunches Danny and I had shared when we were in grade school. I had reconnected with him briefly in high school, but when I moved to the Calhouns' house, we didn't see each other at all. Now that I had my own car and a brand-new Nextel cell phone, I could call him and see him! With that thought in mind, I asked Mr. Swanson for Danny's number just as they were leaving.

As soon as I got out of work, I went through my routine of changing in the front seat and driving to a secluded place before I called him. I was excited as I parked at Vilano Beach and dialed his number. He answered, and we quickly decided on a place and time to catch up. I told him I'd had some bumps in the road and was staying on Vilano, just a few miles from where he still lived. An hour later, he met me at the beach. I didn't want him to know I was homeless, and I had never been so thankful for my tinted windows. I hopped out of Sunny and ran to his jacked-up, bright blue Dodge Ram truck. We drove to the edge of the water and talked for hours as we stared out at the ocean waves.

"Danny, I'm so glad to see you! Tell me everything I've missed. Girlfriend? Or should I say, *girlfriends*? How are your parents? You know I saw them today. Your little brothers too. Y'all look just the same. Not one of you has changed."

I was overjoyed as I caught up with my childhood friend. I whispered a thank-you to the Lord as we talked. Danny was just as nice and easygoing as ever. All was the same between us, just as it had been when we were growing up. He told me all about his girlfriend and the fishing charters he did with his dad's business.

It wasn't long until Danny figured out that I was living in my car and started bringing me food. Well, technically, it was Mrs. Swanson who was sending the meals, but Danny delivered them. Soon, I started parking outside their house, just as I did on occasion at the Jabours' house (Jay's parents) or at the house of my other friend from Smoothie King, Li-Sha. Both Jay and Li-Sha helped me out as much as they could when I was homeless.

My closest friends and their families were kind and gracious to me, never once making me feel unwanted or shameful. Jay called me every day to pray with me. Always encouraging me in the Lord, Jay was just like Danny and Li-Sha in that they all believed I had something worth fighting for—something grand in my future. Danny's and Jay's parents treated me like one of their own and invited me to stay over and enjoy meals with them whenever I wanted. Although I rarely slept over at my friends' houses or ate with them, on the occasions when I allowed myself to say yes, I had such a nice time. Whether it was Li-Sha and me feeding all her lizards and giant pet tortoises or Jay and me sitting in his truck eating ice cream and talking about Jesus, I never wanted for anything when I spent time with my friends.

Months went by. I saved every penny I could to put a deposit on an apartment. By this time, I had left Village Inn and started at Sangrias as a server and bartender. I worked day and night—as much as they'd let me. Work a double shift, shower at the beach, sleep in car, repeat. Finally, after months of squeaking by, I had enough money. The day I got the keys to my first apartment, I was beside myself. After almost a year of living in my car, I didn't know if I was dreaming or simply delusional.

Was this really happening?

The woman who rented me my two-bedroom, two-bath Vilano Beach condo was from a church I had recently started attending. The rent was $950, so the deposit was twice that amount. Even though I had struggled, my time in Sunny created in me a depth and perseverance I wouldn't otherwise have had.

On the day I was to move in, I met my new landlord at the condo and wept tears of joy as she handed me the keys. Unaware of my current plight, she looked at me, confused. I never told her I was living in my car, because I was afraid she would change her mind and refuse to rent to me.

So there I was—keys to my very first apartment in hand!

Lord, we did it! We really did it!

Crying with relief, I put the key in the lock and opened the door. I kicked off my flip-flops as I stared into a bare-bones but beautiful space. I took one deep breath. Then I took off like a jet, running through the entire apartment. I was laughing and crying as I ran my hands over every wall and rubbed my feet into the new carpet.

Bliss. Absolute bliss.

I ran up the stairs to my loft bedroom and saw the most

glorious thing of all—a shower. And not just any shower, *my shower*! Mine, all mine. I could sit in it all day long if I wanted to! I ripped open the shower curtain and discovered the most beautiful skylight overhead. The sun and clouds were right in the shower with me. I cried even harder after this discovery. I couldn't believe it. After months of dirt under my nails, nappy hair, and grimy feet. After salty and sandy everything from showering at the beach. After just getting fired from Village Inn for dirty uniforms. After all that, I finally had my very own shower. Talk about a dream come true!

Oh, the joy of being clean! I never knew the sorrow of dirt until it ravaged my femininity and robbed me of my dignity. Now clean water was all mine for the taking, and I didn't have to endure the shame of asking a friend again. I didn't have to pretend to go surfing so I could use the shower at the beach. No one would wonder what I was doing.

No more paranoia.

No more embarrassment.

I ran to my car and brought everything I had inside. I placed all my possessions smack in the middle of the living room. It was amazing. All 900 square feet of it. After unpacking, I was off to bathe beneath the skylight with the beautiful sun and clouds overhead. I brought all my girly things to my bathroom and turned the shower faucet to warm.

So bright, so beautiful, was that bathroom!

With tears in my eyes and a grin on my face, I put out my hand to feel the water. As it washed through my fingers, I felt instant peace. The moment had come. Satisfied with the temperature, I took off all my clothes as quickly as I could. With one foot poised over the side of the bathtub, about to feel hot, clean water for the first time in months, I thanked the Lord.

Thank you, Jesus. Thank you for this beautiful shower. I don't know of anyone else who's gone from living in a two-door car to living in a 900-square-foot Vilano Beach condo. So, again, Lord, thank you!

When I stepped beneath the flow of running water, a wave of contentment came over me. That water felt so good, so warm, so clean. I stood in that shower for hours.

I will never forget the feeling of that first shower washing over me and making me new. It's the renewal that was so beautiful to me. I was a girl again. I had clean hands, clean feet, clean hair. I felt like I could fly. My hair was soft, and my skin was glowing. I wasn't dirty or ugly anymore. I was in every sense lovely. And for the first time, I truly believed it.

That afternoon, Danny came over with his parents, bringing me food and blankets. Jay drove up from Daytona, and we lay on the carpet in my bedroom and talked about the faithfulness of God. I'd recently joined Good News Church and its Bible study group, and a few friends I had met there came over that night too. We all prayed together in joyous thanksgiving for this victory. Jay was very proud of me for making it through a tough time. "You are the strongest girl I know," he said. "You can do anything!"

I took his words to heart and tried my best to become something and someone worth being.

I was still an avid surfer, so most mornings I put my board under my arm and walked across the street to the sunlit ocean. This day, I had been surfing all morning, taking a break only to drive to A Street after hearing that the swell had picked up by the pier. It was a local hot spot. It was hard to get in the lineup, especially as a young woman who didn't know how to do any tricks. I was a longboard surfer who could paddle out and catch a few waves, but that was about it. I was only there to ride the wave peacefully.

After being in the water all day, I was sunburned and hungry. It was a little after 5 p.m., but I decided to ride one more wave and then come in. It was just so beautiful!

I paddled out, and what happened next was awful.

Out of nowhere, a wave rolled over me and sent me barreling into someone who was riding a wave.

I panicked. I did all I could do to get out of his way, but I got caught up in the roll. It sent my feet overhead into the swell. My board flew above me as I tried to get above the roll of the ocean wave.

After the wave passed, I made it above the water, gasping for air. I could see shore, and I tried to swim.

Nothing.

My arms moved, but not my legs. A cloud of red blood surrounded me in the water. Panic again flooded my body. Something had happened to my legs. They were completely limp. I couldn't feel them, couldn't move them.

Lord, please don't let me die out here!

Another surfer swam toward me as I began to drown.

As he dragged me out of the water, leaving a trail of blood in my wake, I looked down and saw a giant piece of flesh protruding out by my right hip, just below my bikini line. Down to the bone, veins, ligaments—I could see it all.

Had I just been bitten by a shark?

He placed me in the sand and prayed over me as a crowd gathered around us. Shock had taken its toll. All I could do was say the name of Jesus. I repeated his name over and over. The EMTs gave me shots of something that knocked me out. I woke up in the hospital covered in blood and sandy from head to toe. I tried to move my legs again.

Nothing.

A doctor came in to tell me what had happened. The fin of my board had stabbed me in the thigh, missing my femoral artery by just one centimeter. It was a miracle I was alive. She said the numbness in my legs was from shock. Although several nerves were severed, she believed I would just lose feeling in my right leg but eventually be able to walk again.

Miracle!

As the doctor began to stitch up my thigh, I told her all about my friend Jesus. He had been saving me since childhood. He was always keeping me from the edge of death. Her eyes widened as she silently worked on my leg. I'm pretty sure she thought I was one of those crazy Bible thumpers, but she listened politely as I gushed over the love that God has for us.

When the doctor discharged me the next day, Mr. and Mrs. Swanson came to the hospital to take me to my apartment. Mr. Swanson is a six-foot-six, 290-pound rugged fisherman, so he had no problem scooping me off the gurney. He carried me to their truck and placed me in the back seat. We made a quick trip to CVS for my medication and then drove straight to my apartment. Mr. Swanson gently carried me to my bed while Mrs. Swanson found some towels to put under my leg. Like a true mother hen, she went right to my fridge. Once she saw the empty shelves, she quickly set off to Publix for groceries.

The road to recovery was trying, to say the least. For weeks, other people had to help me bathe, use the bathroom, and raise money to help me pay the bills until I could go back to work.

It was my worst nightmare.

Relying on others was absolute torture for me. I hated taking anything from anybody, let alone accepting help for so many basic things. But it was during this season of trial that I learned the importance of community. I also learned that having pity on someone and caring for them are two different things. Just because someone cares for me doesn't mean they pity me.

When Mrs. Swanson insisted on filling my fridge with food, it was an act of deep compassion, not pity. So I let her cook meals for me. I accepted Danny's offer to stay with me most nights until he had to leave for his stint with the Coast Guard. He changed my bandages and helped me get to the bathroom. I looked forward to Jay's weekly visits when he would pray over me and bring me smoothies. I was grateful when my Bible study group raised money for my rent and other essentials so I could heal in peace without fear of losing everything I had worked so hard for. These people did all this out of love and empathy. They tended to me because they saw a need they could fill—and did fill—with great care, I must say!

What would I have done without these precious people who were there for me in my times of great need? I was "Spike" when Danny first saved me from a few wretched little girls in the lunch line. I was a senior in high school when Jay gave me a job at Smoothie King, only to find out that I needed a lot more than a job! What would I have done if he hadn't driven me to school in that Smoothie King van?

Now this! The Swansons and Jabours were a real family to me, and they were kind without ever expecting anything in return. They simply saw my needs and met them without one thought for themselves. What would my life have been like without them?

God, in his infinite wisdom, placed me in the path of some of his most loving people.

God reminded me that free will is a gift. Even when someone decides to abuse their gift of free will to harm another, there are still plenty of people who choose to use their free will to do good. God is not the author of violent or hateful acts. He is the God of love. *He is love!* We are not robots, pulled by strings on a whim. We are humans. We are free to say, do, believe, and feel whatever we want. How should we use this ultimate gift of free will from our Creator?

It would have been impossible for me to heal if the Swanson and Jabour families had not sacrificially loved and cared for me. Good News Church helped too. Pastor Andy and his wife, Kristy, were so loving and kind. They gave me money to pay my rent and other bills until I could walk again. How wonderful to have a small community of human beings to help me when I was in need! From bedridden to wheelchair to crutches to walking to running, I made it through—thanks to my new family.

After three months of healing and getting back into the swing of work, I decided I wanted to move to Jacksonville Beach, about twenty miles up the coast. I was about to embark on a new chapter in my life. I couldn't wait to spread my wings to see where they would take me.

> Until the time came to fulfill his dreams,
> the LORD tested Joseph's character.
> *Psalm 105:19 NLT*

CHAPTER 12

Ms. California

I made enough money working double shifts as a bartender in St. Augustine to save for a rainy day. Life was mostly moving along as normal when one night, my little sister Jemma called me out of the blue. She was crying hysterically and told me someone had tried to attack her in her dorm room. She had called Mother and several others, but no one could help her. I was her last resort. It was the middle of the night, but I immediately set out on the six-hour drive to Miami. I helped her pack up her dorm room, and we headed back to my apartment in St. Augustine.

A few weeks later, Jemma and I moved together to Jacksonville Beach, about forty-five minutes away. I managed to land a lucrative bartending gig at the Lemon Bar, world-famous for its lemon bar freezes. The floor was sand, and the view was the ocean. The ocean bar was attached to a hotel, so in the mornings I worked as a maid and then walked over to make drinks throughout the night.

Jemma and I had a cute apartment just one block from the beach. Although I had stopped surfing after my near-death experience, I still loved walking on the beach every day and swimming in the water when it was calm. My sister surfed competitively, so our location was ideal. I worked double shifts five to six days a week. I picked up shifts others didn't want so I could save money for us. We were living the dream. We always had groceries in the fridge and AC in the summer. Who could ask for more?

During this time, I found a new church, Beaches Methodist, led by Pastor Joby Martin. It was here that I became involved in a women's small group Bible study and met a woman named Lori, whom I affectionately called Momma. (In fact, I still call her Momma.) From the first day we met, Lori treated me like the mother I always needed. She's helped me make every major decision and continues to be a mentor to me. She has been a huge influence in my life, and I love her very much.

Over the next several months, I settled in to life in Jacksonville Beach and I wanted to help Jemma do the same. When I found out about the Jacksonville Beach lifeguard program and shared the information with Jemma, she was excited to participate. So I paid for her to take the summer course, which she passed with flying colors. She then became a city employee as a Jacksonville Beach lifeguard.

I was so proud!

Jemma and I grew very close. Our time together wasn't without struggle though. Jemma is a free spirit, so she chafed against all the rules she had to follow when she lived under my roof. No alcohol and no boys. But oh, how I loved mothering her. I'd make her a lunch most days and drive to the lifeguard station to drop it off. Her smile was ear to ear when I handed her the lunch. I was thankful to have the means to offer something, and she was grateful to have someone care about her.

Jemma's surfing improved every day, giving her opportunities to compete on the semi-professional circuit. She even secured a sponsor, and her entire world revolved around lifeguarding and surfing. My life was centered on taking care of us, being involved at church, and going to the gym. I trained to compete in some local races, such as the Trident Never Quit triathlon, and took my best shot at bodybuilding. Jemma and I kept our noses to the grindstone, working day in and day out, but we couldn't satisfy the itch to move. We brainstormed and eventually made a decision to get the heck out of Dodge.

We were California bound! We could find a better future there, right? Create a life of dreams—or so we had heard! Plus, from California, Hawaii was much closer, which would be great for Jemma's surfing career.

So we did it.

I moved first, and Jemma came not long afterward. California was a strange place for a girl who'd only been outside of north Florida for ROTC competitions. Driving across the country awakened my soul to the joys of travel. I saw things I had literally never seen before. The mountains in the rearview mirror revealed to me my true size—how small we are as humans, and how frail. As I journeyed on, I felt a strong sense of determination to write my book and to start a nonprofit for abused girls in Los Angeles. I knew that Florida and California had the largest populations of foster youth in the country. I would be in a prime location to help the forgotten children of America.

And so began the grueling path to achieve my dreams in the City of Lights.

I found an apartment in Venice Beach and quickly got a bartending job at the Venice Whaler, an iconic bar on the beach. I also quickly realized that people here weren't as kind as people back home. Venice Beach was a giant melting pot of people who all wanted great fame and fortune.

None of that interested me, so I found friendships outside the entertainment industry. And I found a new church, Core Church LA. Once again, I joined the women's Bible study, which is where I met one of my best friends, Megan. I also found plenty of new friends at American Defense Enterprises, a world-class small arms weaponry training range nestled in the mountains in Burro Canyon, where I took classes. On my days off, I loved target shooting at the range or hiking all the trails and summits in Southern California. Hiking alone in the mountains gave me a sense of wild abandon and freedom from the world. I had never fully adjusted to city life, but I felt happy and free when I was hiking all the southern peaks or shooting at the range. I stuck out like a sore thumb most places I went, but California soon gave me the opportunity of a lifetime.

I'd been in California for about seven months and was finally beginning to feel settled. I was grocery shopping at Whole Foods in Santa Monica one afternoon when a well-dressed man approached me. He had luxury written all over him, from his sunglasses to his Italian leather shoes. Immediately, I judged him. *Typical LA, living-the-life-of-the-rich-and-famous guy.* I also assumed he was hitting on me.

I was dressed in a casual ankle-length purple sundress, and he stood in front of me, openly looking me up and down. "You should compete in the Miss California Pageant," he blurted out. His voice was matter-of-fact, his body posture confident.

"Excuse me," I said, "have we met? I really don't think I'm the gal for that, but thank you so kindly." I quickly turned around to walk away.

This man has lost his cotton-pickin' mind. Pageant? I don't think so. I laughed to myself at the thought, but he approached me again.

"No, seriously," he said, handing me his business card. "You should try out. The link is on my card. Call me if you change your mind." Then he walked away.

I stared at his business card, certain he was either insane or desperate for a date. I brushed off the encounter, threw the card in my handbag, and continued shopping.

It's said that curiosity killed the cat. Well, curiosity surely was digging its claws into me, so the next day, I got on my computer, googled the web link on his card, and began gathering intel. This Miss California United States Pageant was a big to-do! It was a competition, and a hard one at that. I started toying with the idea of being crowned a queen.

What does that mean exactly?

Where do I find a gown?

Do I have what it takes to walk around in front of thousands?

Does it mean I win money?

Could I launch my nonprofit?

Could it help me with my book?

Do I have what it takes?

What would it mean if I competed?

I wondered if I had the grit to do it. A trigger went off, and Mother's words swirled around my thoughts, silencing my go-getter mind-set.

"You're a whore!"

"You're only good for one thing!"

"You'll never graduate. You'll never go to college. You can't even read."

After drowning out the memories of Mother, I wrote down all I needed to do in order to compete. Gowns. High heels. Entrance fees. Outfits for every event. Makeup. It was a daunting list of hundreds of things I needed and didn't have, including "mandatory community service." Community service was a huge part of winning the crown.

What have I done, and what would I do if I won?

Oh, I knew exactly what I'd do if I won. The exposure would

be a boost to help me launch a nonprofit organization for foster care youth.

It was then that my heart cried out, *Yes, you can surely do this!*

After mulling it over for days, I concluded that God, in his infinite wisdom, was offering me, a tomboy from the South, an opportunity to become Ms. California, United States.

How silly! Me? A beauty queen?

But oh, how wonderful to have the platform to reach others!

Over the next few weeks, I went to work on checking off the items on that daunting list.

I first had to win a local pageant, so I filled out all of the paperwork for that. I wrote an essay and sat for an interview. After a few weeks, I was selected to be Ms. Ventura. This paved the way for me to compete in the state competition five months later.

Now the real work began.

I had to raise thousands of dollars to be in the competition, so I hit the pavement. I told everyone who'd listen that I wanted to compete for Ms. California on the platform of reforming foster care. I was strong in my convictions and confident I could make a difference. Business after business sponsored me.

I met with the man who had recruited me in Whole Foods. After talking with him, I realized he was a kind man and not at all the person I had initially judged him to be. Judging a book by its cover is an injustice to both the book and the reader. After all that I'd suffered because of the way I looked,

I should have known better. But I began to learn that the more I listened with my ears and my heart, the less there was for my eyes to judge.

The beauty of humanity is that we are so unique! Each of us is given a set of gifts that perfectly aligns with our purpose. Whenever I rushed to judgment and dismissed a person based on their appearance, it seemed the Lord was right there to show me something magnificent about them. I no longer wanted to miss out on a good conversation or a personal connection because I let my eyes do the judging before a word was spoken.

After two months of relentless effort, I had raised close to $10,000. I borrowed gowns, shoes, clothes, and makeup. It was real. I was going to take my shot at being a pageant girl! I spent hours upon hours practicing hair, makeup, and walking on stage. I practiced answering questions and googled videos of previous pageants to glean anything I could to better prepare myself.

When I won Ms. Ventura, I met a woman named Ms. Kay. She owned a dance studio, and I went there to learn some moves. Through Ms. Kay, I met Ms. Bee, who also happened to have the means to sponsor me. Together, these two women became a strong force in my life. They believed in me more than I believed in myself. They helped me with everything— gowns, shoes, makeup, bathing suits. They taught me to dance and gave me voice lessons. For the interview portion of the competition, Ms. Kay stitched me up in a dress suit straight out of Ms. Bee's wardrobe from the 1950s. I looked like a million dollars.

What a gift they were!

Months of preparing, practicing, and rehearsals made way for one very special day. I was nervous, excited, and scared, but above all, I knew I was on an important journey. After being beaten, tortured, and ridiculed for not looking like my parents or siblings, here I was using those very same physical attributes to launch a new, positive, life-changing adventure.

God is truly a miracle worker.

When I showed up on day one for the Ms. California United States competition, I saw a sea of amazingly beautiful, well-put-together girls. Each one seemed to have a personal assistant, mother, and cheerleader. I was way out of my league and I knew it. But there was no way I was turning back. After all, it's hard to beat someone who doesn't quit, so at least I had that going for me!

Looking back on it now, the competition itself is a blur, but I remember the impact it had on me with crystal-clear clarity. For years, I was rejected, despised, and ridiculed with names fit only for a monster. My soul had cracked right down the middle. Words have the power of life and death in them. I went years without hearing my given name at home. Which is why even to this day, the most beautiful sound on earth to

.ne is the sound of someone saying my name. Every time a person calls me by my name, my heart weeps with relief.

When the pageant emcee announced my name as the winner, as the new Ms. California, I didn't hear the roaring of the crowd. I didn't jump at the sight of the sparkling diamond crown placed on my head. I didn't cheer myself on for claiming the title. Not one of those things moved me in that moment.

I wept at the sound of my name.

Christina Meredith

Redemption had come, and now the whole world knew my honest-to-goodness name.

I was crowned Ms. California on April 13, 2013. Ms. Kay was there on the front row. After my crowning, one of the judges ran onstage, grabbed my arm, pulled me close, and said, "You earned every gem in that crown. I believe that you will change this nation, one orphan at a time. Give 'em hell, Christina."

I cried for joy. I cried for me, yes, but I also cried for the others I would now have a chance to help. Thanks to the crown, I had a platform on the world stage for building my nonprofit, the Christina Meredith Foundation. My mission? To give girls like me the tools they needed to climb out of the miry pit of poverty and abuse.

The next year was a whirlwind of charity events, red carpet premieres, and galas. I gave TV interviews, was a guest on radio talk shows, and traveled on speaking tours. I was the opening presenter for the 2015 Special Olympics in Long Beach and spoke at more than one hundred events for foster youth. I had private audiences with some of the most powerful men and women in the world. I went hunting with the former secretary of state, James Baker; ate dinner with Jeb Bush; met with California senators Dianne Feinstein and Barbara Boxer; and spoke to other members of Congress about the plight of foster children. I traveled all over the country, speaking to thousands about overcoming adversity and about the realities facing aging-out foster youth. I even had the honor of speaking to an auditorium full of students at my former high school. My NJROTC mentors—Gunny Hanson, Captain Young, and Master Chief Duffy—were all there to behold the growth of a young girl they had helped raise. It was by far my favorite event.

Wherever I went, I shared words of encouragement and stories of hope with my audiences. I started blooming in my twenties! I was like a wildflower that had been wilted for decades but had now finally sprung to life with hope.

Shortly after winning the state crown, I began my fund-raising efforts to compete for the national title, Miss United States, which is held in Washington, DC, on the Fourth of July. I was serving as Ms. California and working part-time, so the days flew by. Still, I managed to raise thousands for everything I'd need, from designer gowns to spray tans. The national competition was much more intense, with more "on" time that required more poise, more perfection, more everything. The pageant was also televised, which added another layer of pressure. As a competitor, you couldn't leave your hotel unless you looked like absolute perfection. At all times, you had to be perfectly put together and ready to smile for the cameras.

When I didn't take home the national title, I felt devastated for a few days. But that feeling quickly waned when I realized God still had a purpose. He had given me a once-in-a-lifetime experience that was filled with lessons I needed to learn. And that in itself proved to be more than enough.

There are some lessons you just can't go to school for. Engaging people in diverse circumstances helps a person grow. Being tossed into situations that don't seem to mean much in the grand scheme of things can sometimes become an indispensable stepping-stone. This experience on the pageant circuit helped me know my boundaries. It helped me see both the positive and negative aspects of women competing for a crown. There were many important ways in which the competition helped me grow as a person and paved the path to get me to where I am today. And I am forever grateful.

A few months after the national competition, a newspaper in Los Angeles published an article about me. It just so happened that an entertainment producer named Betsy Kennedy read it. Betsy is very involved with nonprofit work, and she sent me a lengthy email about a public service announcement she was producing on behalf of foster care children. She wanted me to be the spokesperson for the campaign. I immediately said yes!

My first impression of Betsy, whom I affectionately call Bets, was that she was a brightly burning light. Her smile was wide and sincere, and her beauty was exceeded only by her gracious demeanor and kind words. She was magnificent to behold. I was mesmerized as she shared her heart for others and especially for foster youth. I instantly wanted her to mentor me.

Betsy was the perfect person to help me navigate the treacherous waters of the entertainment industry. She had grown up in the wealthy Brentwood community, graduated from Stanford with a degree in film, and helped produce several major motion pictures. Do I even need to say how brilliant she was? I also discovered that we shared a mutual love for the beautiful Jesus Christ. I loved her heart, and it wasn't long before we were speaking every day, plotting ways to tackle the foster care crisis.

Not long after we met, Betsy introduced me to a man named Brad Freeman, who knew her parents from their college days together at Stanford University. Mr. Freeman was a sixty-something good ole boy from Fargo, North Dakota. After attending Harvard Business School, he began his investment banking career in Los Angeles and in 1983 cofounded Freeman Spogli & Co., a private equity firm.

Betsy told Mr. Freeman about me and explained that I was looking for a place to stay while I started college and worked on my book. When we officially met in person, he asked me what I planned to do after completing my term as Ms. California.

"Mr. Freeman, I'm going to write a book, and then I'm going to reform foster care in its entirety."

He looked up from his comfortably worn sofa and without hesitation said, "That is very shrewd of you, Christina. You're welcome to stay here. You can stay in my daughter's old bedroom. My housekeeper will set it up for you."

Mr. Freeman's home was a straight-up mansion in Brentwood. It had a guest wing in the main house, as well as a separate guest house in the lush backyard.

What Mr. Freeman didn't know was that everything I owned was crammed into my two-door Honda Civic. I was once again between places and had resorted to sleeping in my car. I was "shrewd" enough not to tell him!

It had been a rocky few months filled with disappointment and lots of driving. Jemma had moved to Hawaii to pursue her surfing career, so I left California for Florida and stayed there for a couple of months, hoping to get a book deal. When my book proposal was rejected, I returned to California to figure out what I wanted to do next.

Mr. Freeman had no idea the hopeful young woman in his living room was homeless. He simply gave me the passcode to the front gate and told me I could move in the next day. I drove away with tears in my eyes as I prepared to go from the poorhouse to the palace.

The first time Mr. Freeman and I had dinner together, his dining room table was formally set for two, and the housekeeper served the first course. I looked at all the silverware, the china, and the napkin perfectly folded and set on my plate. I knew he knew I had no idea which fork to use, so in his gracious, no-nonsense manner, he said, "Outside in. Always remember that." *Oh, yes, indeed!* Manners I had, but etiquette is learned from environment, and I was being trained correctly and with care by Mr. Freeman. Any time we had a conversation, he would—and still does to this day—correct my English. He is the ultimate grammar police! But I'm not complaining. In fact, I'm grateful for all this man taught me during the months I stayed with him.

While living in Mr. Freeman's guest room, I worked diligently on my book. During one of our conversations, I'd expressed my desire to get into politics later in life. So once again, Mr. Freeman helped pave the way for me. He was going to a dinner with his best friend's brother, Jeb Bush, as Mr. Bush was toying with the idea of running for president. Mr. Freeman took me to this event, introducing me to everyone he knew. He told them about my book and about all I had accomplished as a homeless youth. He sounded a bit like a doting father as he pointed out all my achievements and goals for the future. This was a humbling experience for me because I so badly wanted to make him proud.

As I sat at dinner with several of the wealthiest men and women in the country, I couldn't help but chuckle to myself. *My bank account has less than $200 in it. How did I end up at this table?*

The Lord definitely has a sense of humor! At the start of the evening, I felt mildly out of place, but shortly after our party was seated, I began to enjoy this enormous learning curve.

I realized I was seated with the very people I was supposed to be seated with. I was destined to have every dinner, every meeting, and every handshake. I learned more at a private dinner party for Jeb Bush than I ever learned in a classroom. It just shows the mysterious and miraculous ways of God. He can take me anywhere he wants to take me.

Nothing is too hard for God. Nothing is impossible!

After my reign as Ms. California ended, I went on to speak all over the country. I shared my story everywhere, from churches to universities. I was declared a hometown hero by the city of St. Augustine. The same city that had caused me so much heartache in my childhood, now recognized me in an honoring way, allowing me to find healing through acknowledging my past. On April 1, 2014, I was privileged to speak at a meeting of the county commissioners in St. Johns County, where they issued a proclamation designating April 2014 as Child Abuse Prevention Month.

The mayor of St. Augustine invited me to be the honored guest at the annual Nights of Lights ceremony, where he shared my story with more than ten thousand people. They all applauded my victory before switching on millions of holiday lights.

The Florida Department of Children and Families invited me to speak to hundreds of children around northeast Florida, including state-funded youth foster homes, the Duval Regional Juvenile Detention Center in Jacksonville, Communities In Schools of Jacksonville, and several other places.

Being crowned Ms. California wasn't just about becoming a beauty queen; it was about becoming a woman who could give back to a hurting world.

> Hope deferred makes the heart sick,
> but a dream fulfilled is a tree of life.
> *Proverbs 13:12 NLT*

CHAPTER 13

Purpose

In my experience with pageantry, I found that most women who claim the crown don't plan for what they will do after their sparkling, yearlong reign is over. The day after I won, I knew I didn't want to end up with nothing after I crowned the new queen. I prepared for what was next. I wanted to catalyze real change for real people. I wanted to make a difference.

I began writing proposals for my book, putting together business plans for my nonprofit, and taking every opportunity I had to speak before an audience. I listened more and spoke less in conversations with others. Cultivating my listening skills helped me grow as a leader. I spent a great deal of time reading Scripture and was constantly in prayer. I heeded all the advice my mentors gave, even when I didn't like it. This was key to staying on the straight and narrow and making progress toward my dreams.

Each door that opened brought me to another door. When doors closed, I allowed them to shut, even when it was painful or confusing. I trusted that whatever was given to me was from above, and I accepted it with thanksgiving. In the dark seasons, I remembered the dreams God had given me during the year I lived and slept in my car. *I would write a book. I would speak to thousands. I would be a beacon of hope for the suffering. I would serve my country!* And so I continued to work tirelessly to achieve the goals I had been diligently working toward for years.

My first victory, or so I thought, was when a small publishing company said they wanted to work with me.

At last!

However, after spending thousands of dollars to visit them and work with them on writing a book proposal, they decided I wasn't a good fit and dropped my book from their roster.

I was devastated.

I had come so close. I'd had an agent and a publishing house. *How can this be?* I cried out to God in confusion. But I refused to be defeated by rejection. I would stay the course, no matter how daunting it looked. Despite countless rejection letters from agents and publishers, I continued to seek publication—for years. I read each rejection letter with optimism, trusting that God had the very best plans for my story.

While living with Mr. Freeman, I continued working at the bar, taking on odd jobs, writing my book proposal, and saving as much money as I could. It's very difficult to survive in LA without some help, so I was very thankful for Mr. Freeman's kindness and generosity. After staying with him for about seven months and starting school at West Los Angeles Community College, it was time for me to move on.

At this point, it had been about two years since I'd been crowned Ms. California. Betsy once again helped me find a safe place to stay when she introduced me to Henry and Tori Cloud. In addition to opening their home to me, the Clouds helped me to heal and grow—and they helped me turn my dream of writing a book into a reality.

Henry, a world-renowned psychologist and author, took me under his wing. He helped me sift through memories of my years of abuse and guided me to the right agent and publisher for my book. His wife, Tori, showed me what it looks like to be a loving wife and mother, as well as a no-nonsense business-woman. As I watched how the Clouds lived and related as a family, I knew they had what I wanted. Two loving spouses who were raising children together and creating a home full of beauty and welcome. They were as open and loving to me as Lori, Betsy, Jay, Mr. Freeman, and the Lord above.

I believe my entire journey to this point has been divinely led, and that God continues to orchestrate my path. Even when I'm stretched to the point of quitting, I remember that trials are not about me; they're about learning to press in for the greater good of others.

When I finally landed a book deal, I took several months to hide away and write. I unplugged from social media.

I limited my commitments and stepped back from being overextended and being "on" at public events. I needed more time to heal from childhood wounds. Still working on my college degree, I moved back to a little Florida town outside of nowhere—Polka, Florida, which has a population of fewer than a hundred people. We have one blinking traffic light, a Dollar General, plenty of farms, and tons of hunting land.

After almost five years of living in busy LA, working part-time jobs, and doing ridiculous amounts of travel, it was a dream come true to seclude myself in a charming old farmhouse in the South for a few months to write this book. Experiencing trials makes peaceful times so much more beautiful.

My focus now is on fulfilling my purpose. I have many goals and dreams, but they can all be summed up in one sentence: *My burning passion is to fight for the oppressed, to love people with a feverish zeal, and to serve others sacrificially.* I want to do this by pushing for reform of the foster care system in its entirety and by raising awareness of the global pandemic of sexual abuse. I hope to set the captives free. If reforming foster care and ending sexual exploitation are my goals, I must practice selflessness. And so I am constantly asking myself questions like these: *How can I help the hurting heal from crippling wounds, and how can I stop the evil ones from harming other human beings? How can I love well those whom God has placed in my life? How can I love the oppressed* and *the oppressor?* Above all, I want to love in the way that Jesus loves, with a love that is not of this world.

I know this will not happen overnight. Learning to love like Jesus takes a lifetime. It goes against the me-first human impulse: *What's best for me? What do I get out of it? How will this affect me? I don't want to love this person if it requires sacrifice. I'll help as long as it doesn't cost me anything.* Most of us have been taught to put ourselves first, but this way of living only robs us of joy and intimacy in our relationships. I want that joy and that intimacy, and so I am committed to my purpose. My purpose is driven by my desire to change the lives of others for the better, to live out a love that is the polar opposite of the hatred that dominated the house I grew up in.

Sometimes I think of it this way. The world does not owe me anything; it is I who owe the world. I owe it my talents, gifts, time, attention, and sacrifice.

Who is the world?

It is you!

You are the world to me. Every single human being is the world to me. My purpose is to help those who are suffering. To forgive the unforgivable. To lead others to the life they dream of. To extend a hand to the unloved, unwanted, and uncared for. I value each person as sacred.

You have been God-breathed into this world with great care. It does not matter where you were born, what religion you claim, what color your skin is, what sexual orientation you are, what shape your body is—nothing matters except your very being. God formed you in your mother's womb, and that means you are to be honored as sacred.

Because, dear heart, you *are* sacred.

You are to be cherished.

Loving a broken world is the privilege and the purpose of every Christ follower. We are called to love the unloved, to be hope to the hopeless, to be light in the darkness. To fight for justice, no matter the cost.

What is *your* purpose?

Every human being has a purpose—a reason for being. Do you know what yours is?

At night, when you're alone with your thoughts, what do you dream about? What never stops whispering to your heart? What do you want to make beautiful? What do you want to create? That is the thing you are meant to do. You have a passion for this thing for a reason. Explore this passion in a God-honoring way. Have you seen someone go through life without purpose, without passion or zeal for anything? It's painful to watch. Don't let that happen to you.

Purpose can be anything—anything that sets *your* heart on fire.

Even when I was little, I was driven by my purpose to protect and seek justice. My blood boiled with righteous indignation as I watched Mother or Herman dole out punishments to my siblings. My mind is filled with memories of painful scenes—my younger siblings covered in bruises, wincing as they tried to sit down. The sound of their tummies rumbling from a lack of food. Memories such as these fuel my mission to set the captives free. To help the oppressed become the bright lights of the world. To usher people into extravagant hope. To fight for what is right and to ensure justice for all people.

After traveling across the country and speaking to thousands, I have heard many stories of horrendous abuse from innocent children and young people. Stories that might make you hate humanity. Stories that might cause your heart to ache with physical pain. Stories that might make you want to give up in despair. But it's these very stories that embolden me to press further into my destiny. I refuse to give up, and so I will stand up for those who are beaten down, and I will stand between the innocent and the evil whenever and wherever I can.

I will work to create a firestorm of awareness about sex trafficking, pornography, and all other types of sexual abuse until it's no longer acceptable to casually write it off with statements such as, "Well, that's just the way the world is," or "Boys will be boys."

I will work to end the aging-out process for youth in foster care and to find loving homes for every child in the foster care system.

I will work to provide mental health services for those who have survived sexual, physical, or psychological exploitation.

I will work to educate and help communities from within, and to end the cycle of poverty and abuse that devastates families.

I will work to remove the stigma of trauma so that no one who has suffered abuse has to carry the additional weight of shame, a weight that crushes the spirit of a person who wants to create a beautiful life.

Impossible?

No! Nothing is impossible for those who believe in their God-given purpose and who work in God's strength to fulfill it.

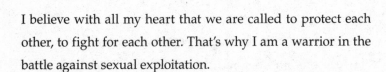

I believe with all my heart that we are called to protect each other, to fight for each other. That's why I am a warrior in the battle against sexual exploitation.

There is nothing more soul crushing than sexual abuse. It is a vile act in which one person steals the body of another and violates the sanctity of another beating heart to satisfy a perverted pleasure. It is inhumane; it is torture; and it is nothing short of evil incarnate. There is nothing on this earth comparable to the sin of sexual abuse. It rots the souls of those who have been betrayed.

If you have been violated by the sin of sexual violence, hear me when I say that you can be made whole again. I can tell you from my own experience that this is true. Healing from the wounds of rape or any form of sexual exploitation is a long and painful journey, but thank God, all things *can* be made new—including me, including you. Your joy can be fully restored.

I started my healing journey at the age of thirteen when I told my two best friends what had happened to me. My healing

continued when I stuck with it through years of trauma therapy and countless moments of allowing myself to acknowl-
edge and feel the torment of having been so brutally violated.
Healing is painful. Healing is work. But the fruit of this healing labor has been oh so sweet.

That's why my heart is heavy with the burden to remind
every person, and especially every victim of abuse, that they
are sacred.

God made you.

You are valuable.

You are worthy.

And you are oh so loved!

I want to scream it from the tallest building and shout it
from the rooftops! Hear what I am saying to you and believe it:
You are worth the sacrificial love of another. You are worthy!

If you've cried while wondering why that person used you
and then threw you away, know that your tears are not only
valid, but they are precious and will not be wasted. We were
not created to use and abuse one another; we were created
for deep, intimate, meaningful relationships. We are meant
to love and to be loved. That love is meant for you. No abuse
disqualifies you or makes you unworthy of love.

Just as I am a warrior in the battle against sexual exploitation,
I am also a warrior in the battle to protect children in foster
care. In the United States, there are currently more than 400,000

children who are wards of the state. Due to abuse or neglect at home, they are placed in the custody of the government of the state in which they reside.

What does it mean to be a child in the foster care system? To put it mildly, it means you are up a creek without a paddle.

It means no normalcy or stability.

It means packing your meager belongings into a stylish black trash bag and moving to a new home every other month or even every other week.

It means you've probably only been to the dentist once or twice in your life.

It means your one meal a day at school will not be made with Mama's love or include heart-shaped sandwiches.

It means you will most likely suffer sexual abuse, violence, and poverty.

And once you age out of the system, it means becoming an adult long before your peers, even if you're still in high school. While other kids your age are obsessing about dating, summer vacation, or what college to attend, you're working a second shift at Denny's, covered in days-old ketchup because you don't have access to a washer or dryer. It means that when you get your paycheck, you have to decide whether to pay your rent, buy groceries at Walmart, or save money for a taxi to get to school so you can graduate.

I was nine when the Department of Children and Families started knocking on our door. I was ten when people began reporting the bruises and my reclusive behavior. It wasn't until I was sixteen that my five siblings and I were, finally, officially removed from Mother's custody. At that point, I knew that graduating from high school was a life-or-death situation. It was my only hope of survival. I didn't want to end up as a prostitute, like Mother always said I would, or dead in an alley due to an overdose—also something that Mother always threatened would be my fate. Even though I had resolved not to give in to the cycle of poverty and abuse that had crippled my family, meeting the demands of everyday life was still an uphill battle.

I wanted normal. I wanted PTA meetings after school and barbecues after church on Sunday. I wanted a loving family. When I aged out of the system at eighteen, I kept pursuing my dream of normal the best I could, with just what I had. I didn't have the luxury of being irresponsible or carefree like my peers who were applying to colleges and making grand plans for their future.

The fact that I graduated from high school was nothing short of a miracle. College wasn't an option for me at the time—not because I hadn't given my very best to get there, but because I was a good girl who'd been dealt a really bad hand. I was trapped in a system that pushes children down rather than sets them up to be as successful as their peers who have had stable home lives and loving parents. Eventually, I did overcome my hardships—with my own hard work, help from good Samaritans, and the love of Jesus—but not every child in foster care is able to do the same.

So who are these children in the foster care system? Allow me to paint a picture by sharing a few facts:

- Children in the foster care system are 44 percent Caucasian, 23 percent African-American, 21 percent Hispanic, 10 percent other races or multiracial, and 2 percent unknown race or ethnicity.[1]
- While in foster care, children will experience an average of eight home and school changes.[2]
- Approximately 20,000 to 25,000 children a year age out of the US foster care system at eighteen. Twenty percent of them will immediately become homeless.[3]
- About half of those who age out will graduate from high school with a diploma or GED, and only 3 percent will go on to earn a college degree.[4]
- Within four years of aging out, 60 percent of the boys will be convicted of a crime, and 70 percent of the girls will become pregnant.[5]
- Nearly 50 percent of those who age out will struggle with substance abuse and unemployment. Thirty-three

---

1. US Department of Health and Human Services, Children's Bureau, Child Welfare Information Gateway, "Foster Care Statistics 2016," www.childwelfare.gov/pubs/factsheets/foster/.

2. First Star, "First Star Foster Youth Academies," www.firststar.org/wp-content/uploads/2015/02/First_Star_Trifold_small.pdf.

3. National Foster Youth Institute, "51 Useful Aging Out of Foster Care Statistics," May 26, 2017, www.nfyi.org/51-useful-aging-out-of-foster-care-statistics-social-race-media.

4. National Foster Youth Institute, "Education: Foster Youth Face a Special Set of Challenges outside the Classroom That Have a Serious Impact on Their Academic Performance," www.nfyi.org/issues/education.

5. Family Equality Council, "Economic Security and Youth Aging Out of Foster Care," www.familyequality.org/_asset/k4xs1c/ECDF---Economic-Security.pdf; see also Mark Courtney et al., "Midwest Evaluation of the Adult Functioning of Former Foster Youth" (2011), www.chapinhall.org/research/report/midwest-evaluation-adult-functioning-former-foster-youth.

percent of boys and 75 percent of girls will receive government benefits such as food stamps to meet basic needs.[6]

- Twenty-two percent of aged-out foster youth battle with post-traumatic stress disorder (PTSD), which exceeds the rate of PTSD in the general population by five times.[7] This surpasses the rates of veterans who served in Iraq and Afghanistan, 12 percent of whom are diagnosed with PTSD.[8]

There are plenty more grim statistics such as these to bring grief to our hearts, but I think you get the point. Aging out of the foster care system effectively swings a young person into other systems, such as prison and welfare. And by the way, the brokenness of foster care costs taxpayers $80 billion a year due to its egregious failures and consequences.[9]

So why is this catastrophe allowed to continue? The sad reality is that the cause of foster care reform is neither

6. National Foster Youth Institute, "51 Useful Aging Out of Foster Care Statistics," www.nfyi.org/51-useful-aging-out-of-foster-care-statistics-social-race-media.

7. Molly O. Fechter-Leggett and Kirk O'Brien, "The Effects of Kinship Care on Adult Mental Health Outcomes of Alumni of Foster Care," *Children and Youth Services Review* 32, no. 2 (2010), 206–13, www.nysnavigator.org/files/professionals/effects_of_kinship_care_on_adult_outcomes.pdf.

8. Richard A. Kulka et al., *Trauma and the Vietnam War Generation: Report of Findings from the National Vietnam Veterans Readjustment Study* (New York: Routledge, 2013); Charles W. Hoge et al., "Combat Duty in Iraq and Afghanistan, Mental Health Problems, and Barriers to Care," *New England Journal of Medicine* 351, no. 1 (July 1, 2004): 13–22.

9. Richard J. Gelles and Staci Perlman, "The Estimated Annual Cost of Child Abuse and Neglect (April 2012): A Prevent Child Abuse America Report," www.firststar.org/whats-at-stake/facts.

glamorous nor compelling enough to gain national attention or to merit a place on the priority lists of most of our nation's leaders and politicians. In fact, our leaders have, sometimes knowingly, made decisions or created systems that only perpetuate the cycle of poverty and abuse for hundreds of thousands of children down through the generations.

How can we bring solutions to these problems? How do we take on what I consider to be the biggest civil rights crisis of our time on behalf of a minority who can't vote, can't rally in front of the White House, and have no viable recourse? We fight for them, one issue at a time. And by we, I mean you and me. We can fight for the least of these—and we can enlist others to help.

I know the problems of the foster care system may seem impossible to fix, but fixing them *is* possible.

I also believe it's possible because I've met amazing people who are fighting these battles already and winning. Let me share just one example. First Star (www.firststar.org) is a national nonprofit committed to tackling the education crisis for foster youth. Their goal is to fix the educational divide so that the graduation and success rates of foster children match or even surpass those of the general population. To achieve this objective, First Star has launched youth academies for high school foster youth in fourteen universities throughout the country.[10]

Each academy is a four-year program designed to show

---

10. First Star, "Our Academies," www.firststar.org/our-academies.

foster youth that they, just like their peers, belong on a college campus. Youth live on a university campus each summer throughout their high school years and return to the campus one to two days each month during the school year. As a result, the university becomes almost a second home and students have the opportunity to build supportive relationships that enable them to dream big and achieve big. The program gives foster youth access to the very best role models—their peers in college who are already successful in pursuing their education.

How's this for amazing—100 percent of the foster youth who complete the four-year First Star program graduate from high school. This is a statistic that makes my heart so happy! And there's more good news. Forty-six percent of First Star twelfth graders go on to attend four-year universities, and 44 percent attend two-year colleges—that totals 90 percent who attend college!

First Star is proving that foster youth are just as capable as their peers. All they need is the foundation of support, consistency, tools, and love! And not the sentimental pat-on-the-back kind of love, but the kind of love that says, *I'm going to invest all of my time and energy as if you were my child*. It's a comprehensive, wrap-around love that our nation's foster youth so desperately need.

A few months ago while I was speaking at a conference, I got a call from my sister RaeLynne. She and I were the only ones among our eight siblings who hadn't spoken to Mother in more than a decade, but RaeLynne had recently been in contact with her.

HOW YOU CAN HELP

There are an unlimited number of ways you can help children and youth in foster care, but here are just a few ideas to get you started:

- Invest your time and finances by volunteering and contributing to legitimate nonprofit organizations that aid and advocate for foster youth, such as First Star, Together We Rise, Hope's Closet, and Foster Closet.
- Consider becoming a loving foster parent or adopting a child from the foster care system.
- Partner with the Christina Meredith Foundation (www.ChristinaMeredith.org) to ensure that any youth who has experienced abuse or is in the foster care system receives basic necessities, education, trauma care, health care, and advocacy.

We each have our own battles to fight to make our world a better place. We also have a responsibility to help children in need. My hope is that you will engage in your passion and live out your purpose—and also prioritize taking concrete steps to help make life better for others.

RaeLynne was so overwhelmed by what she was about to tell me that she could barely get the words out. Here we were, almost fifteen years after officially leaving Mother's home, and something unbelievable had just happened to one of the most powerful men in St. Augustine.

After all eight of us kids left Mother's house, Herman, Mother, and their two boys lived the life they appeared to want—a life without any of us. But RaeLynne told me that their two boys, my half brothers, had been flagged as victims of child neglect by the Department of Children and Families in St. Johns County.

According to my sister, Mother told the Department of Children and Families that Herman had been abusing their two boys. She then went to the next county over, Volusia County, where Herman had a condo and no family or law enforcement ties, and filed charges against him at the sheriff's office there. I couldn't believe it. The man who'd worn the shiny badge in St. Augustine was himself arrested and booked in the county jail one town over on allegations of abusing my half brothers. The Volusia County Sheriff's Office wound up dropping all the charges she filed against him for reasons unknown to me, but Mother and Herman remain engaged in a battle over his rights to see my younger half brother (my other half brother recently turned eighteen) in a case that feels eerily familiar to what happened to me and my siblings all those years ago.

See how the cycle of abuse and dysfunction continues? We must work to fix this injustice.

As for my father, I never witnessed him raise a hand to Mother. I believe my father's downfall was loving her too much—so much, in fact, that he lost all his children. He protected her before he protected us. He lives with this every day, regretting his decision to stay with a woman he believed was mentally unstable and abusive toward his children.

After all I've been through, would you be surprised if I told you there is room in my heart for mercy and forgiveness? I do not pine away, hoping for doom and gloom to come to those who have hurt me. Not at all! In fact, I hope they'll hear my voice of forgiveness and be made well through God's grace, therapy, and a dose of reality. With so much heartache in the world, it would be a waste of my precious energies to harbor ill will against those who have wronged me. Unforgiveness is a cancer to the bones. It rots *you* from the inside out, not the one who has wronged you. It may take years for you to see the harm that unforgiveness has done to you, but in time, hate will rob you blind. It will leave you hollow, bitter, and destitute. Why would I want any of those things in my life?

When people who have been deeply wronged tell me they can't forgive because it feels like letting the one who wronged them "get away with it," I tell them that forgiving those who hurt you doesn't mean they shouldn't face the consequences of their actions. God, in his infinite wisdom, has given us the order of law. I'm a hearty supporter of our governing laws. If someone does the crime, they should do the time. Period. So, I heartily support both forgiveness and consequences for actions.

Can you imagine a world in which there were no consequences, no matter the action? How frightening!

When we forgive others, we release them into the care of
God. Only God can pardon a soul. This is not our task. We can
offer forgiveness, but we must not confuse forgiveness—setting
others free from their offenses against us—with taking away
the consequences for their actions. When it comes to commit-
ting crimes, a perpetrator may not always be caught, but hear
this: What is done in darkness will eventually come into the
light. Jesus taught that there is "nothing concealed that will not
be known or brought out into the open" (Luke 8:17). And there
will be consequences for harming children. "If anyone causes
one of these little ones . . . to stumble," Jesus said, "it would be
better for them to have a large millstone hung around their neck
and to be drowned in the depths of the sea" (Matthew 18:6). In
other words, it would be better to be tied to a concrete block
and thrown into the ocean than to wound a child in any way.

If you come from a childhood of abuse, know that the Lord
cares for you and that it wasn't his will for you to be abused. It
was man abusing free will. Be encouraged—you don't have to
let it cripple you. You can learn to forgive. You can find healing
and be set free to live out your purpose.

Do not take revenge, my dear friends,
but leave room for God's wrath, for it is written,
"It is mine to avenge; I will repay," says the Lord.
Romans 12:19

CHAPTER 14

Suffering

Suffering is an unavoidable part of the human experience. If someone tells you that all you have to do is a, b, and c and no harm will ever come to you, you're being sold a bill of goods. Demand your money back and run away as fast as you can. Each of us will at some point experience loss, heartache, trauma, depression, anxiety, and misery. Suffering is not reserved for just some people; it comes to us all. Sometimes it comes at our own hand, and other times at the hand of another. However it comes, I encourage you to accept this fact of life rather than try to resist it or avoid it. In fact, I encourage you to embrace the idea of suffering, because it *is* coming—with or without your permission.

If you are in the midst of great hardship in any form, know this: the trial you are enduring may well lead to your purpose or be the stepping-stone that enables you to achieve greatness. Have you ever read heroic stories of those who overcame seemingly insurmountable odds? Or cheered for those who have suffered great loss but persevered and claimed victory in the end? Or rooted for the underdog? If so, then you have what it takes to be the hero in your own story—to overcome, to persevere, to be the underdog who beats the odds.

If we are willing, even the most severe suffering can produce character in us—the kind of character that emerges only from the fires of intense grief. Great duress forms unwavering integrity. Insurmountable odds create unshakable convictions. Dark nights of the soul give birth to a humble heart.

Suffering is not sent down from God above to crush us frail humans. It is a gift in disguise that unlocks the hero within us.

Whether your suffering takes the form of sickness, grief, or violence isn't what matters most. What matters most is knowing that you *can* find safe ground again and a renewed purpose after pain has swept you off your feet. You can write the next chapter in your story in any way you wish. You can be the underdog who doesn't quit, no matter the cost. With every decision you make, you can choose to be the hero—or not. Never give up on your God-given purpose!

My suffering took many forms. One of the most devastating was being raped by my uncle for many years. God didn't do this to me. I do not shake my fists toward heaven, cursing the Almighty for my wounds. A man took his free will and used it for evil instead of good. Do I believe that God could have slayed my perpetrator in the act at any moment? Yes, I surely do. I don't know why God didn't intervene, but I trust him. I have a rock-solid faith in his unending love for me, and I believe he can do all things. Which means that nothing is impossible for those who believe. Small and big miracles happen every day. I also know this: all of my suffering in the end has brought me to this place—a place of victory. I am the hero in my own story because I have hope and a purpose.

I am afforded opportunities today not because of a privileged upbringing, but because of all the unbelievable grief I bore. Trust me when I say that suffering does not have to be a dead end. If you're willing, it can be a door that leads you into a whole new life.

It's not hard for me to write these words now as I sit in a cozy farmhouse miles away from civilization. No one is more thankful than I am to have this moment of peace. There are no words in the English language to articulate how deeply grateful I feel simply for this moment. *All of my suffering has enabled me to enjoy life—to relish it for the precious gift it is—a hundred times more than I would have if I'd never suffered.* A simple walk outside among the trees, the hug of a friend, a meal from my fridge, a shower at any time—the smallest things are my greatest joys because I know what it is to suffer.

Bad times deepen our capacity to thoroughly enjoy the good times.

Nothing can prevent pain from entering our lives, but we must never give up hope. God is for us, not against us. When the seas of life rage, he can tame the winds, calm the waters, and bring us safely back to shore. We must not fear doomsday, but boldly live our daily lives with hope. We do that when we allow suffering to do its perfect work within us, drawing us into deeper relationships with others and with our Creator. My most cherished bonds were formed under great stress. Jay, Betsy, Lori (Momma)—these extraordinary humans kept my world from falling apart when all hell seemed to be breaking loose. When I was bearing heavy burdens, I intertwined my hands with theirs.

Who I am as a woman, sister, friend, and leader has been shaped by my adversities. I have credibility, not in spite of what I have endured, but precisely because of what I have endured. Who wants to hear about hope or overcoming difficulties from a person who has never struggled?

Suffering is a door that opens to a world of purpose.

Our heartaches can have meaning. Even when life takes every opportunity to crush us into powdered ash, we can choose to look ahead, beyond our current circumstances, beyond the anguish we feel. We press into pain with great expectation, knowing that at some point, the pain will cease. Remember this when you're experiencing deep despair. In time, things *will* change.

My years of suffering were measured in decades, but God took something horrendous and made it into something good. How many children, young people, and adults have I encouraged by sharing my journey the last few years? Enough for me to say that my CinderGirl childhood was worth enduring. I believe that with all my heart. It is an honor and privilege to bear the burdens of grief with others. It is my greatest joy to tell others who are suffering that their wounds can be healed, that they too can be filled with hope. I believe that we all have a story to tell, and that God wants to use our stories to empower others—to usher in a global movement of healing and positive change.

It is my greatest desire to take away the suffering of the world. I'd take away your suffering if I could. I hate seeing another human being in pain. I can't shield you from suffering, but will you allow me to encourage you—to tell you that life isn't over after a savage blow knocks you to the ground? You can get back up and fight. You can persevere. You can seek light amidst what seems to be crushing darkness.

I can't shield the world from suffering, but I can work hard in my little corner of it to ensure that those around me are offered fundamental human rights. I can work hard so that abused children have viable options for healing, so they can grow to be healthy and whole adults.

I can't rid the world of evil on my own, but I can join hands with you and others to face it head on. There are countless ways that we, together, can help our fellow human beings to overcome evil and suffering.

The system that failed me as a child is the one I've now dedicated my life to fixing. I have chosen to fight the good fight in the hope that one child at a time will hear my voice and believe that they too can overcome their sufferings. I pray that the flame blazing inside me will ignite a flame within the heart of every suffering child—that they will hear the still small voice of hope and believe that their lives can and will be redeemed from the ashes.

Master Chief, my NJROTC mentor, liked to give me a reminder after every cross-country practice and drill meet. He stood on the sidelines of the Nease High School track in his khaki uniform, posture strong, balancing his coffee mug and clipboard while barking out orders.

"Rugrat, get over here! Listen to me now, okay? Listen well. You listening?"

"Yes, sir, listening. Ears on, sir!"

He leaned in toward me, eye to eye. His voice was firm but not unkind.

"You can dream anything," he said. "And anything you dream you can achieve. You play like you practice. Practice hard! You're a bright one, Rugrat. Don't let anyone dim your bulb, you hear me?"

I've never forgotten what Master Chief told me, and I never will.

The Spirit of the Lord God is upon me,
because the Lord has anointed me to
bring good news to the poor;
he has sent me to bind up the brokenhearted,
to proclaim liberty to the captives,
and the opening of the prison to those who are bound.
Isaiah 61:1 ESV

Epilogue

Today I'm serving in the United States Army as a National Guardsman. I'm participating in the Simultaneous Membership Program as an enlisted soldier and a contracted cadet to be commissioned as a US Army officer.

Serving our great nation has been a dream of mine since I was a little girl. I'm so beyond the moon that soon I'll be an officer in the United States military. It reminds me that I'm capable of achieving anything I dream.

It reminds me that although this dream took more than fifteen years to become reality, there's something to be said about never quitting, no matter the setbacks or detours.

I travel the country frequently as a speaker for foster care advocacy and mental health, specifically trauma healing and care. Sharing my heart on the truths of healing after trauma and abuse is a real need in our communities. The more we talk about mental health and the need to take care of our minds like we do our physical health, the healthier our families and communities will be.

It also brings me great joy to lobby for the complete

reformation of the foster care system. We are doing a great disservice to our nation's future by not tending to our foster youth like they are our own flesh and blood. I'm confident that my efforts will achieve small victories in both of these areas, which will allow for a ripple in the hearts of others to hop on the train that puts our families and communities first.

I work diligently to accomplish my goals and never allow myself to feel self-pity for very long when things don't go my way. I believe this has helped me shake the dust off when people or life bring me to my knees, and it empowers me to press forward toward my goals. I have created what I call the four Ds. These are words that now shape my daily existence: *dignity, decorum, discipline,* and *discretion.* I'll share what each of these words mean to me, as I believe words have monumental power over our bodies and minds. This is why I always choose to speak *life* over myself and others. Words shape our very lives. This is the rock-solid truth.

Dignity is not allowing myself to behave in a manner that cheapens my self-worth or value as a person. I will not sell myself for a quick reward that comes from losing my moral code. I hold myself to a standard. Deviating from this standard for anyone or anything interferes with my integrity and can surely bring more harm than good to my conscience.

Decorum is important as a woman because I want to behave in a manner that leads young girls and women into a place of good taste and modesty. Proper etiquette is essential in every aspect of life. These attributes should be learned and practiced every day so we are always putting our best foot forward in every situation.

Discipline is essential to any type or amount of success. Self-control is my number one practice. I work on this muscle memory daily. I actively work on physical and emotional discipline in all that I do so I am always ready for the task at hand and always able to make sound, reasonable choices. Without discipline, we can't achieve anything small or great. This skill set should be harnessed with daily mindfulness and great care. Practice makes perfect, and self-discipline is an attribute that will never go out of practice!

My final word for daily living is *discretion*. As a public figure, this is a constant balancing act. It is essential to keep your inner personal struggles and hardships close to your inner circle and not air your dirty laundry for the world to see. The world is not equipped to hold you up or help you up—that's what your small circle of trust is for. Discretion is also important when it comes to other people. Keep your words out of others' business. It's better to be thought a fool for staying silent than to be thought a fool when speaking. Do not despise silence; it is truly a gift. I encourage you to practice listening more and speaking less more often.

I also continue to spend a lot of time with the Lord and reading my Bible. Every day I'm in Scripture, and all throughout the day I am hollering at Jesus. This is just a part of who I am. He keeps me, and I keep him, busy!

Recently, I launched my nonprofit, the Christina Meredith Foundation, which helps foster care youth and abused youth climb out of the sandpit cycle of poverty and abuse. Advocacy for trauma care for every foster child is another giant portion of my reform policy, which I will continue to fight for undeterred until it is accomplished. My foundation allows me to travel and speak truths to those who can help make tangible changes for our foster youth.

I want readers to know I still struggle with trauma, and I'm still on my healing journey. I still have good days and bad days, but the good outweighs the bad. I work on myself every day. I take great care in learning how to love those around me and to communicate effectively to better serve the needs of those in my world. I make the effort every day to be a better human being.

I want you to know that every single human being on the planet struggles with something. We are all fragile creatures. The only difference is that some choose to make the effort to work toward a greater calling for the greater good, while others choose to sit in the mess that weighs them down and hold on to the excuses that only cause them more grief.

We are not victims, regardless of who did us wrong, what went wrong, or what we did wrong. You are capable of anything, and you are the only person keeping you from living your best life. Love hard, work hard, and believe the impossible. Because, dear heart, all things *are* possible.

I remain confident of this:
I will see the goodness of the Lord
in the land of the living.
Wait for the Lord;
be strong and take heart
and wait for the Lord.
Psalm 27:13–14

Acknowledgments

More than a decade ago when I was living out of my car, telling myself all the reasons it was impossible for me to write a book, it never occurred to me that God had already sorted all of that out. He had a plan. His plan involved people. Beautiful human beings from all walks of life crossed my rocky road of perseverance to help me achieve a dream.

If I've learned anything in my years of trial, it is the absolute necessity of loyal friendship. Relationship is the reason for being. With that, I'd like to start from the beginning of this journey: the Timmons family, the Jabour family, the Swanson family, Keith and Linda T, Matt K, Buster G, Andy and Kristy H, Kevin and Lea Ann W, Cindy G, Christina and Rachel, Kendall A, Mr. Tebow, Gunny Hanson, Captain Williams, Captain Young, Master Chief Duffy, and Nease NJROTC. I was rough around the edges when you gave me hope, care, and compassion. Words will never adequately express my gratitude. Thank you.

The past few years I have had the honor of intertwining

hands with those who saw in me something worth fighting for. When I was unable to do for myself, these people went out on a limb for me, giving their time, finances, and unwavering support to aid me in accomplishing the completion of this manuscript. Karen and Becky, Karen and Rhonda, Bryan H, Danielle S, Megan and Trevor T, Jane J, Justin C, Bill K, Calvin R, Stephen C, Gina R, Ronald C, Perry B, Bobby C, Bill D, and Sandy V. Without you, I would have never made it. Genuine gratefulness for each of you.

Over the course of this wild journey, I have learned the essential need for mentorship. Wise insight, sturdy leadership, and steadfast support are the only reasons I am still gracefully stumbling around. This inner circle is small. These leaders have spoken into my life concerning monumental and seemingly insignificant life choices, allowing me to become the best version of myself. Without each of them, none of this would be. Each one brings a unique brilliance that permits me to learn and grow during all seasons of life. As this chapter of my life closes and together we begin my next epic voyage, know that my loyal love for you is matched only by my profound reverence for you. You are the reason I can dream. You are the reason I can keep secure footing.

Betsy Kennedy Ryzewicz, Eryn E. Brown, Bradford M. Freeman, Lori L. Lambert, Dr. Henry Cloud, and Tori Cloud—I will forever be beholden to you. Words are inadequate to express my thankfulness.